0284 1

SITTING IN JUDGEMENT

ULRICH SIMON

Sitting in Judgement
1913 – 1963

AN INTERPRETATION OF HISTORY

London
SPCK

First published 1978
SPCK
Holy Trinity Church
Marylebone Road
London NW1 4DU

Printed in Great Britain by
Billing & Sons Limited
Guildford, London and Worcester

ISBN 0 281 03572 5

For Anthony and Elizabeth Mellows

And he did that which was evil
in the sight of the Lord.
2 Kings 15.28

And you all know security
Is mortals' chiefest enemy.
Macbeth iii.5, 32-3

Non sien le genti ancor troppo sicure
    a giudicar . . .
(Let not the people too securely sit in judgement . . .)
Dante, *Paradiso* xiii, 130

E voi, mortali, tenetevi stretti
    a giudicar . . .
(Judge, then, you mortals with restraint . . .)
Paradiso, xx, 133

Nie treff' ich, wie ich wünsche,
    das Mass.
(Never do I strike the balance as I would wish.)
(Hölderlin, 'Der Einzige')

CONTENTS

PREFACE

All our yesterdays have been reviewed by a thousand pens in a thousand ways. Never has there been half a century more documented than my chosen era of 1913–63, from the year of my birth to the assassination of President Kennedy. Historians have often collected the data and, in the modern fashion, refrained from evaluating them. A few historians, however, have indulged in wrapping up the events in their ideological dogma. Marxist interpretation has come to the fore during this half-century. But orthodox Marxism has to contend with heretical deviations too. Some writers mix their ideology with a strong and even eccentric individualism, if only to make money or a reputation, however fleeting. For example, the great popularizers (A.J.P. Taylor, etc.) engage in great shunting operations so as to get the factual pieces in a position they like to be known by. Thus, inevitably, autobiography gets mixed up with the unfolding of the spectacle. After all, the genius of Tolstoy blazed a trail of *using* history for a didactic purpose, as in *War and Peace*.

This book is also about war and peace and it also reflects a strongly autobiographical stance. But it is not my intention to write the story of my life. Rather, I intend to sit in judgement so as to bring out, if possible, a Christian evaluation of God's strange work in our times. Theologians generally fight shy of this task, at least in our times, probably because the story they would have to tell is not at all pleasant and not often to their credit. Let the reader sit in judgement with me, for unless we sit or stand above and outside events they threaten to swallow us up. This work is a therapeutic exercise which endeavours to steer the human tragedy into the orbit of the divine comedy.

June 1977   ULRICH SIMON

THE SEAMLESS ROBE

When I set out on my voyage of discovery I little knew that
God would come into it. I had never heard of theology. Nor
did I wish to stir from the hearth at home where I was happy.
It was no hearth, in fact, but central heating, for I was born
into a world of modern comfort. Our apartment in Berlin-
Grunewald was part of a house which had been built at the
turn of the century. Its solidity surrounded me whenever I
felt uncertain or moody. We inhale confidence with the air
we breathe at birth and feed optimism into our system with
the milk we suck at our mother's breast.

No muse answers me to sing the splendour of Berlin or the
greenness of the forest in which these villas stood after the
English style. Poets' incantations celebrate the marshes elsewhere, describe the domes and pinnacles to the south and
west, curse the misty autumns which rise out of the ditches
of the river bed. But Berlin on the Spree has no history beyond the fishing village of the eighteenth century and even its
royal connection points to Potsdam some twenty miles to the
west. Berlin arouses no nostalgia. If it is sentimental it is so in
a cynical manner, for its inhabitants are realists and they pre-
fer the new to the old. Here people gather from other parts
of the world to work and to succeed.

And yet the muse ought to inspire me to praise both place
and people, for unknowingly both thrive in the air which has
no equal. When I was born it was clean and despite the chimneys to the north and east the dry winds cleared the sphere
with a freshness which still amazes me. It could be very cold
and also very hot (no school on those days!), so cold in fact
that I would cry with pain, and so hot that the tar melted in
the streets. But if I were Virgil I would still praise this climate
for its energy. There was a power in this flat sandy city
whose inhabitants were never tired. My father was no worker in
the ordinary sense of employment, but he was at his desk before

we children came to breakfast. My mother administered an empire of activities. Day and night enrolled them and everybody in work and pleasure. Perhaps if I were Virgil I should extol the people because they united work and pleasure so perfectly.

But I am being unjust, for my Virgil would miss the deeper levels which work and pleasure concealed. The poet of the *lacrimae rerum*, however, would not have been deceived by the air. He would have sensed below the energy and the functional comfort a sadness, a melancholy, a questioning, a turbulent 'Why?' which was asked in the sharp tones of ice, snow, and heat-wave. I heard it not at first, for I played on the carpet, under the grand piano, with my mother's laughter in my ear, my brother's interest at my side, in the nest of great security. If I were to sing of childhood I should repeat the minstrels' love songs, the soldiers' marching tunes, and Christmas carols, for life was made up of good women who kissed one, and presents under the lit-up tree.

Ah, but the soldiers! How did they fit in? They came into our home from outside, for despite our privileged position even my mother could not prevent their being billeted upon us during the first years of the First World War. I welcomed them with open arms, for I loved climbing on their broad backs. A grenadier with immense moustaches carried me and I played with his tunic when he set me down. He was unlike my father in appearance and smell. My father was clean-shaven at the time when our armies defended the fatherland in France and Russia. He carried no uniform and never touched a rifle. Even when the authorities scraped the barrel for recruits and all my uncles, however myopic, were posted to look after balloons or field kitchens, the medical examinations stopped when my father came before the army doctors. They took one glance at this strange musician, so thin and unworldly, and would not even accept him for the military bands. Thus the war passed us by in Berlin, except for a gleaming Zeppelin stationed overhead. The smell of our guests in uniform seemed to change and so did my attitude to them. I now cried when they said good-bye, and some vanished even without a word of farewell. No soldier ever returned or wrote to me. I began to sense a secret — the transitory nature of all meetings.

While I was trying out my first steps with the men in field-grey their betters were declaring their ideas of 1914. Ninety-three famous men claimed that this German war was a moral struggle and that the redeeming mission had sent the Germans, not to expand, but to defend the sacred soil and to spread the health-giving German spirit for the cure of nations. I heard soon echoes of 'Gott strafe England', the nation of shopkeepers that needed to be corrected. War was to be recognized as the trigger of true love in a world made soft and corrupt by money-grabbing individuals. But the metaphysics of conflict, underwritten and proclaimed by intellectuals and given solemn authority by theologians, did not penetrate my nursery.[1] All I noted as the years went by was the diminishing gaiety of the soldiers quartered on us. And their stay became too short to favour a familiar relationship.

The war did not interfere with my safety. My nurse wove her kind severity into a heavenly fabric of God and his angels. The system above seemed to correspond very agreeably to my needs below. It was particularly reassuring to have a second father in heaven, who seemed more ready to listen and work on one's behalf than the man whom I liked but could not really understand. This God father had the further advantage that he looked after everybody, or at least delegated his kindly protection to his special angels. Nurse's indoctrination induced every night a feeling of incomparable warmth. Since the prayers made allowances for parents, brother, friends (but never enemies!), I felt the pre-established harmony of the universe in the unbroken web of the stars outside and the family in the home.

Our generation still knew the seamless robe, though the firing in the trenches never stopped. Nurse never failed to mention our soldiers, so that even they were enclosed in the

---

[1] Cf. Fritz Fischer, Germany's Aims in the First World War, pp. 155 ff. — 'Deutsche Reden in Schwerer Zeit', Berlin, 1914. — H. Kohn, *The Mind of Germany*, 1961, pp. 297 ff. — The text of the 93 eminent men is not easily found, though always quoted as if well-known. I traced it at last in the *Basler Nachrichten* of the 7th October 1914. The 93 address the *Kulturwelt* and refute charges of war guilt, violation of Belgian neutrality, brutality and criminal conduct on the part of the troops. Goethe, Beethoven, and Kant are invoked at the end of the appeal: they are as sacred as the people's hearth and soil.

providential well-being, whatever happened to them. Even more important, no feeling of shame or guilt could ever stain our souls, for the day's sins were quite simply offered as inevitable, and with the same inevitability they were forgiven, through prayers and an act of verbal contrition. It was certainly this God's *métier* to forgive sins: he did it every night. Consequently one did not sin very much, for having accumulated no resentment or unconscious guilt, there was no need to smash or destroy anything, nor to quarrel with one's brother, or anyone else. I remember only one bitter conflict with my older brother: we both claimed possession of a sand-castle, when we were holidaying on the Baltic coast during the summer of 1917.

It was a dark year and its despair penetrated even the consciousness of a four-year old. My first experience of alienation coincided with a long wait at the Lehrter station in Berlin. Though it was summer outside the gloom of winter seemed to prevail on the overcrowded platforms. I got separated from my mother, who had asked me to look after the luggage. Suddenly I was overcome with panic. A train with wounded soldiers and sailors came into the station, belching smoke, and as it ground to a halt the first casualties were being unloaded. I saw blood and I smelled disinfectant. Heads swathed in bandages contrasted with the smiling face of the grenadier who had given me rides. The platform grew more crowded and the legs above me threatened to trample me down. Until my mother returned, tickets in hand, I had to wait, and the wooden carriages in front of me and the swirling smoke above, hissing angrily, and the shrieking, grumbling, pushing chaos of humanity around me, have become enshrined as a frightening portrait of the fiend. I found that I could not even pray. The angel had taken flight. The seamless robe had received its first tear. I cried throughout the journey to the Baltic and only retrieved my peace of soul when my brother ended the quarrel over the sand-castle by nearly splitting my head with a spade. My mother took me from my nurse and washed my wounds. I was happier than before.

But the wounds of war were not so lightly received and healed. I saw the retreating armies in 1918. We were in the Black Forest, for despite the breakdown in transport and food supplies my mother insisted on holidays in the country. Outside Freiburg, above a place called Hinterzarten, the long trails of dissolving regiments marched, and we were told that peace would follow war. I reckoned that the God, who, according to my nurse, was with us, must be changing sides. I wept about this for a while, but submitted to his will. I noticed that Nurse did not submit quite so readily but resented the divine decree, which, of course, became a fact in November, when we were back in Berlin. She decided to leave us, and my mother entered my life without a mediatress. She said that the loss of the war was a good thing, and I comforted myself that God had done the right thing after all.

However, when I became a schoolboy I realized that my mother's doctrine clashed sharply with that of my teachers and all the pupils. The school was in the Grunewald and infants and juniors had a building to themselves. Every classroom had a religious motto which could be seen from the street, for over the windows there were Gothic inscriptions, such as 'Concord', 'Modesty', 'Chastity', 'Reverence', and, above all, 'Faithfulness'. Though pacific in intention it soon became plain that these abstract virtues could be interpreted in a martial spirit. The children whose fathers had never come back from the war responded eagerly to a consolotion of revenge and accepted their teachers' distillation of Christian ethics in terms of warfare. We played at war and saw to it that the Germans beat the French and the English.

If it had not been for this fuel the religious instruction at school would have been a very dull business. There were still creeds to be learnt by heart and the catechism was recited in monotone. Words like Creator, Son of God, Blood of the Lamb, embalmed the drowsy class and mixed with the smell of pine, sweat, and soap.

My own religious feelings revived out of school and in the countryside. I had been very ill during the influenza epidemic and felt very weak. Face to face with the mountains of the Kaiser, near the Austrian border, I graduated from Nurse's system of prayer, merit, and reward. The God of the beaten but regrouping German army and navy was also left far behind. Even the cradling touch of the family was no longer needed. Instead I found an isolated place, a seat on a rocky escarpment, where, especially at dawn and at sunset, I would completely forget my existence and become absorbed in the total source and sustenance of life. I spent hours in this contemplation without knowing the first thing about its practice. Whenever I now read Wordsworth and partially sympathize with his grieving over the loss of childhood I remember those hours spent with eternity. Was it pantheism? Whatever it was, it contained an intimation of immortality.

Though wordless and undefined, this dimension did not fit the norms of religion so far received. For the latter you had to close your eyes, whereas for the quiet absorption you needed to see. The sight treasured the outline of peaks and the reflection of the light; it responded with a happiness which had nothing to do with duties, prohibitions, and that one word which covered everything: obedience. Yet even this early period of contemplation made its own demands, for it required attention and concentration. It did not make me into a dreamer.

The years after the war did not favour a state of dreaming. After the influenza came the famine. We were almost always hungry. I was a mass of sores. Even in the countryside you could not get food or only at prices beyond our reach. I took my mother by the hand and dragged her from farm to farm. We begged for potatoes and I never lost my love for them. Given milk from the cow, the occasional egg too, you can forget about the rest. But the peasants did not disguise their contempt for us starvelings, and I hated them. The sullen fat women in the stinking yards said: 'Be off with you!' Then I learnt to smile at them and to break down their resistance, praying inwardly 'Give us this day our daily bread!' and some would answer with a flicker of a smile, and milk, eggs, potatoes followed. Then I was content and realized in my way how God justifies his ways to men.

Violence worried me far less than hunger. During these post-war years machine-gun posts were a common sight and the occasional firing not unexpected. There was a bridge in Berlin, separating Grunewald from Halensee, which had to be defended against revolutionaries. The dreaded name of Spartacus could be heard in our circles. Great was my astonishment when an uncle was once heard to utter his wish that these men with red armbands might win. How could this be? Were they not the enemies of God, as we had been told at school? My mother dismissed my queries with a cuddle, and soon the Reds vanished from the bridge. Order and law were restored. My parents were Democrats, as I found out.

Another conflict now came to an unexpected end. We had had a succession of maids and nurses. Servants had become a great problem. They were no longer devoted to the family. They were lazy and dishonest. They always left after Christmas with their haul of presents. My father, who did not even know the whereabouts of the kitchen, was superbly indifferent to the hiring and firing of these girls from the country, who came for the bright lights and rewards of the city. But my mother suffered at their hands. She fought them and lost. But I solved part of the problem, for one of the maids took me to her bed in an attempt to rape me. I protested, informed my mother, and this was the end of nurses and nursery.

Though unsuccessful this attack on my person left a scar. I had known no guilt, nor innocence either. From now on I struggled for innocence, which is not innocence. I suspected that there was a vast secret to be penetrated and that a child's world, such as mine, was strictly provisional. I linked the hunger and the shooting with this attack on my person and then wanted to forget it, and did not succeed. The prayer 'Lead us not into temptation, but deliver us from evil' seemed designed to meet the case, but I was not too sure. Anyway, the abolition of the nurse gave me a welcome chance to make friends with the one surviving maid and to take her part against all critics in the drawing-room. When she married later I visited her and she served me an omelette made with six eggs.

But first inflation exacerbated our hunger, for now money could no longer buy food at all. I gloried in the millions, printed on banknotes, over-printed even on postage stamps. One day my mother sent me to the chemist's to buy cotton wool, which, she calculated, would come to 840,000 marks. I was not handed any marks, but an American piece, a U.S. dollar, which looked all silvery. I rehearsed the change I ought to be given in the shop, namely over 1,000,000 marks, but to my surprise I was given far more. The dollar had risen to 4,200,000 marks on that chilly afternoon in 1923. I queried the business and the chemist gave a laugh of scornful despair. I can still hear it, for it prophesied the doom to come.

Meanwhile, however, the wave of hunger produced an unexpected reaction at school. We were offered food, free of charge. As long as we produced an empty bowl and a spoon the teacher filled it with dollops of porridge. I was old enough by now to make inquiries about this free gift, and the reluctant reply referred to some people called Quakers who distributed the food. I wanted to know more, but our class-teacher shook his head. He had been wounded at the Somme. His colleague, though, took me aside and quietly informed me of some good Christian people who wanted to save our bodies so that our souls might live. I mentioned this to my friends who dismissed the story either as twaddle, because it was not true, or, even more sinister, as an example of bribery. But they ate the porridge, and left me amazed.

The classes of religious instruction also reflected the bitterness of soul which hates to acknowledge a debt. The class-teacher foisted his pain and anger upon the gathering impoverishment in the children's homes. His lessons were by no means boring, for they had a thrust of their own. The biblical stories came to us with an anti-Jewish polemic. Perhaps, he suggested, Germany would be a better place if, say, Cain had not only killed Abel but also Seth. Abraham, he held, should have sacrificed Isaac, as God had commanded, and we should not be in the hands of money-rakers, profiteers, and usurers. He had no doubt where his sympathies lay in the struggle between Esau the hunter and Jacob the swindler. But he went further than that, for his contempt extended to Jesus and Paul. He ridiculed the Sermon on the Mount, and especially the peacemakers seemed to add salt to his wounds. Anyhow, he told the eleven-year olds, the man was a failure, defeated on the cross. Germans had nothing to learn from him, who had been a Jew after all. Nor was Paul any better, rather worse, in fact. Without him the world would never have heard of the Nazarene, but this epileptic, to further his own ends and make good his physical deficiencies, invented the fables of Christ, the resurrection and the ascension, and

8

founded that slave mentality which turned out to be such a disaster in Europe, and specially in Germany. He ridiculed his Christian colleague, who often spoke at the school assembly and poured genuine piety into readings and prayers. His cynical dismissal of all 'that stuff' found a ready response among us. It was then that I first saw how some of the boys carved swastikas into the wooden benches. Many years later I saw this teacher again, triumphant on the battlefield of Tannenberg, where he demonstrated Hindenburg's victory over the Russians in 1914 with the aid of maps. Later still, in 1933 he had come into his own as an Obergruppenführer of the S.S. and in 1945 he was executed in Poland for the murder of thousands of Poles and Jews.

I was deeply disturbed by this religious teaching, for I discovered only then, as did others, that I was of Jewish parentage. We had not practised Judaism at all. True, my father had been known to attend the synagogue many years before, during the high festivals, but we were 'Christians', though not baptized. Others at school were even baptized, for the assimilation of the Jews had not stopped short of the acceptance of that rite. These Jewish Christians were neither more nor less religious than their Protestant peers. Their parents identified Christian belief with law, order, decency, and perhaps an affirmation of classical culture. The younger generation were on the whole indifferent and hardly ever referred to religious topics. If it had not been for the overt anti-Jewish teaching the Bible would have remained a book of stories like any other. But the age of toleration was on the wane. Even the one and only Catholic could not escape censure. Our teacher deemed the routine of going to mass un-German, and the custom of making one's confession elicited biting comments from him. Hesse, the Catholic, blushed to the roots of his hair and remained silent under attack, and his silence impressed me.

But this prelude to what was still in the future ended with administrative measures at school which made for peace. A priest looked after Hesse, a Rabbi after the Jews, and the Christian Jews could, and did, please themselves. They ceased to have religious instruction, while the Protestants carved more and more swastikas on the benches.

The tact of our headmaster Vilmar was based upon

theological tradition. His ancestors stood for Lutheran dog-
matism, Kantian concepts of the good will, practical reason,
etc., fused with Prussian militarism, and a sense of personal
obligation and efficiency. Needless to say, he also smarted as
a former infantry officer under the shadow of the defeat, but
he did not disdain modern educational methods, even experi-
mented with free choice, and, most strangely, welcomed boys
of Jewish blood into the school. The Grunewald Gymnasium
soon acquired a reputation for liberal toleration, even though
some of the teachers, like the later S.S. man, growled. If the
Head knew of this he never showed any signs, and he reigned
with unquestioned authority. Every Monday he presided over
the assembly, and it was then that I first apprehended the
words of Psalm 90: 'Lord thou hast been our refuge from one
generation to another' became part of my mental capital. The
Head seemed to enjoy that 'all flesh is grass', and the assembly,
though sleepy and even uncooperative spiritually, accepted
the truism. Later the sadistic gym-master proved the point by
subjecting us to endless exercises, and, worse, to standing ab-
solutely still, whether in the intense heat or in the freezing
snow. The sufferings, as we were made to crawl to the point
of exhaustion, also gave point to the cry 'How long, O Lord?'
The psalm made sense in every way: the school saw to it. And
when later on a boy drowned in the Halensee and the gym-
master was expeditiously packed off to far-away Brazil I consoled myself gladly that 'a thousand years in thy sight are but
as yesterday'.

Yet this newly found peace of soul was rudely shaken with
the murder of the Jewish-Christian German Foreign Secretary
Walter Rathenau in 1922. This assassination took place in the
Königsallee, only about five minutes' walk from the school
(which is now named after the victim). The murderers, who
skilfully overtook Rathenau's chauffeur-driven open limousine
in their car, opened fire and killed the bearded man, who represented all that was most gifted, civilized, and assimilated
in western Jewry. My mother had often, during our walks,
shown me the villa where he lived with his mother. She regarded him as a genius. The son of the founder of the AEG
(General Electric Company) he had risen to the top both on
the technical and on the commercial side. During the war he

had acted as an adviser, and even the Kaiser had welcomed his counsel. In short, he represented to the state what Chaim Weizmann had achieved in England under Asquith. But unlike Weizmann, Rathenau was a baptized convert to Christianity. He pondered the mysteries of the universe, and he reflected deeply (and not too optimistically) on social questions. He anticipated the horror of the mechanization of the spirit. During the war he had resisted total capitulation, but before his death he advocated a policy of reconciliation and European accord. His success, which had no charismatic appeal to popularity (indeed, very few people could claim an intimate acquaintance, let alone friendship), evoked a bitter loathing for the 'Judensau' (which rhymed with Rathenau), and the members of the Freecorps mowed him down. On the day of the funeral hundreds of thousands of workers converged from their dark streets on the fashionable suburb and vowed eternal vigilance. The Republic and freedom seemed vindicated and the martyr's death not in vain.

Rathenau's death touched me with prophetic force and insight. He was the forerunner of the 'wise man', whom I was to meet in society and in literature. He came to stand for a long tradition of enlightened, but slightly chilling, humanism, the result of a superior brain and a moral detachment, which one could admire rather than love. Rathenau also demonstrated for me that the moral intellect is more vulnerable than the unscrupulous blackguard, since it is evident that 'a submachine gun in the hands of a fool outweighs a wise man's arguments'.[1] I knew even then by an instinct that deep religious issues were at stake. When I was told how he had not feared death, though warned of the danger of assassination, and had written of overcoming death — since mortality was not 'possible', taken the right contextual view —, and that his mother had in his spirit written to the mother of one of the conspirators, not to express her first feelings of seeking revenge but to speak of forgiveness, I had enough food for reflection. I could not know that it was not destined to end in my lifetime.

But the tearful appeal to reconciliation foundered on the

[1] Cf.E.Eyck, *A History of the German Republic*, 1962, vol. i, p. 21.

hard facts of the conspiracy. The murderous intention was not stifled by the grim outcome. There was a dreadful disharmony, not resolved by the martyr's death. I brooded over the life-stories and pictures of these young men who had banded themselves together to kill. A mere boy, well-brought up, rather soft, had been in league with his elders, who pooled their idealism, fanaticism, resentment, technical bravura, need to show off, lust for adventure and fame, in the great undertaking. Here again I sensed a religious secret, for how could diabolical blackmail and intimidation be so closely allied with blond, starry-eyed devotion? What was the real motivation behind these youngsters? I did not realize then how they were being used by cynical employers for their own ends. Nor could I digest their end, when the two young killers were themselves cornered and died, one shot dead while resisting, the other by his own hand. (Later the Nazis erected a monument in their honour, which lasted no longer than their own terror.) The alleged repentance of the chauffeur after his conviction and the story of his aid to persecuted Jews many years later highlights the complexity of this, and every other, murder and conspiracy.

It was then that I first heard the solemn marches, and the elegiac verses of the secular hymns, such as 'Eternal victims', moved me as much as the red flags, mingled with the black-red-gold of the Republic. But this religious feeling clashed sharply with the deliberate silence with which the school acknowledged the murder on its doorsteps. The gym-teacher seemed determined to counteract such feelings as mine with a longer and more exhausting semi-military drill. The majority of the boys sniggered at this death. The only teacher who made mention of it was the pious Flocken, whom the parodists imitated for common amusement. He mourned because Rathenau had been a baptized Jew. Flocken was devoted to the person of Jesus as saviour and accepted the chosen people only because they, or rather the remnant, had cradled the chosen servant. All this was above my head and of no interest to my peers, but like a seed the distinctions remained dormant in my mind.

Two feasts in our calendar took us to the church in the Grunewald, where Pastor Priebe had baptized more Jewish

12

children than anyone else. Young Priebe in my class was always a little embarrassed by the fact, and the word 'Juden-kirche' could sometimes be heard. However, the Feast of the Reformation and the Day of Repentance recalled a different age. The chorals and even the sermon conveyed a feeling of awe. I was amazed and even exalted, but since my emotions were not generally shared I withdrew into a private world. The triumphant 'Feste Burg' did not exist except within, and in the past which was slipping away.

Religious devotion was fading away. But I smelt something new on the odd occasion which had nothing to do with church, or pomp, or school. The Bonhoeffer family invited the children in the vicinity to play in the Toy Symphony, which was then attributed to Haydn. We were handed little percussion instruments, and I had a triangle to manipulate. But my eyes were fastened on an older boy, very fair and beautiful and manifestly kind. This was Dietrich, who shone like a star, distilling in his face the warm, intelligent, and liberal air of his home. Soon I had violin lessons in the same circle and from time to time I saw Dietrich there and also at school, where he was, of course, my senior by several years. His home vibrated with life and happiness, not of an indulgent but of a demanding kind. That it must become the centre of a great achievement through pain no one could have guessed at that time.

2

'WHAT IS CHRISTIANITY?'

The second half of the twenties roared in Berlin with delights
and plenty. War, inflation, famine, sores could now be forgotten, as American credits came flooding into the country. Not
only food came on the table in greater variety than ever, but
cars appeared in the streets. I counted the Chryslers and
Buicks. The shops gleamed with luxuries. But the new materialism was perhaps too new to envelop us. Sport also was not
yet a religion, though football and tennis made headway. I
worshipped Sobek of Hertha B.S.C. and Tilden the American
star, much to the disgust of our older teachers. Their dream of
revenge and military training no longer appealed to youth.

Far more influential, and of lasting impact, was the eruption
of new music, new plays, new literature, new art. It so happened that my home was a meeting-place of the famous and
those who were yet to make their reputation. Klemperer,
Kleiber, Walter, Horowitz, and many other musicians appeared
on the domestic horizon. I watched their arrival behind partly
transparent doors. At these large social gatherings I made
common cause with the maid and counted the tips as the
guests left. Even then I acquired a feeling for the competitive,
if not the seamy, side of this world of entertainment. Not
everyone could be successful, and my father lacked the tough-
ness which ensures public acclaim. I gathered from my parents'
disappointments that life was hard and that the wrong people
often won the laurels. In particular, my father either could
not, or would not, compose twelve-note serial music, and the
name of Schönberg caused many an uproar at home. The war
between the classical tradition and the demolition of antiquity
raged fiercely, and uncomprehendingly I found myself in the
middle between the contestants.

My father was the embodiment of tradition, not only in
music, but also in philosophy. Theology did not touch him
directly, but one day, as we were walking near our home, and

We were at the Bonhoeffers' corner, he said to me: 'Harnack lives there'. Then the famous man was seen to emerge and my father took off his hat and Harnack returned the greeting. I had heard the name, for Harnack was famous not only as a theologian but as a distinguished founder member of the Academy of Science and in the educational world. He was the heir of that Protestant tradition which we still associate with the name of Schleiermacher. Theirs was the endeavour to preserve Christian claims in an age of enlightenment and science. They were not merely establishment figures, but wished to reconcile the old with the new, not only theologically but also socially. Harnack had received many a rebuff in his earlier days, before he became the powerful centre of disparate movements in church and state. The Kaiser trusted him and, perhaps, even listened to his advice before the war. My socialist uncle, not surprisingly, repeated the jibe that Harnack was the man who 'kept the Kaiser's diary'.

When I saw the old man he must have been disenchanted, for the theologians could not so easily creep back into favour with the new republican régime. After all, their 'God with us' had led the armies to bleed to death. Even the nationalists for their part did not like Harnack, for they sniffed at his liberalism and his willingness to collaborate with the Rupublic. The new theologians were not yet well known, and only now, fifty years later, has there been a publication in English of the Harnack—Barth controversy, in which the former defends vigorously and sadly the position of a rational, scientific Christian theology against the suspect radical, who breaks up Christian tradition by contrasting divine revelation with human reason.

Harnack's *What is Christianity?* (which appeared in English in 1901 and again in 1957 with an introduction by R. Bultmann) has had an interesting history of approval and opposition. To this day it remains a masterly summary of an historical interpretation of Christianity. Christ, the teacher of the brotherhood of man, authenticates the value of goodness and the progress of civilization. Even after two world wars this liberal-conservative currency is still accepted in the borderland of ethics. Harnack did not like extremism and warned against the excesses of mysticism at a time when it was hardly a temptation at large. He repeated Grimm's story of the fisherman's wife who prompts her husband to demand home, riches, and lastly divinity, only to be reduced to the original state of utter misery. As a church historian and the editor of the influential *Christliche Welt* Harnack pleaded for a reasonable and workable system and against fanatical perfectionism. He died at the right time in 1930.

But even in the twenties, with no crisis in view, the human spirit stirred in a direction wholly opposed to Harnack's theology. The fisherman's wife could be heard asking for more, be it in atheism, agnosticism, radicalism, or blends of these, in theology. New Testament studies, in particular, tore away the vestiges of old-fashioned belief. While Barth's *Epistle to the Romans* (the commentary was thus given its ironic title by the critics who hated it) still 'rang the church bells at midnight' with its existential challenge and glorying in paradox, Bultmann and Dibelius persuaded their pupils at Marburg and Göttingen that the New Testament was the product of the community and its needs. Bultmann's long essay 'Jesus' 1926[1] remains a beacon of what was then in the future and is now commonplace.

In the twenties Jesus Christ drew the cross-fire of hostile groups. For over a century friends and foes had written biographies, mythical portrayals, and novels depicting anything but orthodox belief. But now the climate ceased to be favourable to Jesus as a person. The questioning became an exposure of the futility of Christian existence, and this, in turn, challenged some New Testament theologians to reformulate the meaning of the Gospel. The liveliness of the debate in the universities seemed to augur well for the future, just as the country recovered from the war.

This new Jesus had to survive all the slurs against the pale Nazarene, the Jewish miscreant, whom Nietzsche and his extreme followers had tried to execrate for ever. He was no longer the humble peace-lover, but a secret individual with a universal appeal. Unknown by all, he had become Messiah and risen Lord. Miracles and exorcisms were ascribed to him by a community of preachers and agents who revolutionized

---

[1] English translation 1934 and 1958.

16

the world. Here was a radical mediator of God's kingdom, who demanded more than he gave. Jesus, in short, became the mirror of a deeply divided world, reflecting our problems and tensions. His name was accordingly invoked by conservatives as well as progressives, whose aims were in direct conflict.

I only heard an echo of these activities, when to my parents' surprise, some of their guests, mostly of Jewish origin, defended differing points of view and clashed over Jesus. Clearly, their Jesus had nothing to do with my nurse's Saviour, nor with the German Christ of the school religion. Their Jesus was mostly against religion, as represented by the churches. He was an outstanding person, perhaps a little naive, but a man who freed himself and others from war in all its forms. He was a Tolstoy, the answer to all our noblest feelings, one who affirmed life by denying the suicidal instincts, so recently exposed by psychologists, and brought again to the west by travellers in the east. This Jesus stood for our social ethics, in which everyone was entitled to a good life. Jesus could become acceptable. But I still remember one evening when this picture was shattered by a passionate young man, a Jew, now a Christian pastor, who denounced this sentimental rubbish as idealistic moonshine compounded of wishful thinking and disposable self-justification. No, the new Jesus, he told the company, was against all idealism and humanism, had no stake in any ethics, and if love figured at all it contained neither feeling nor affection. Obedience, command, demand, surrender, decision: these were the words which finished off notions of progress. 'Hatred of the human race' and not 'banal sympathies', he concluded, came nearer the truth.

Oddly enough, all these contestants appealed to Albert Schweitzer as their unquestioned authority. Liberal pacifists cited Schweitzer as confidently as eschatological radicals. The man began to interest me even more when I heard of his medical work in West Africa. He thrilled my romantic heart, for though I found his *Quest of the Historical Jesus* (which my father gave me to read) too difficult and slightly boring, I loved the final purple passage about Jesus beckoning us as one unknown from the other side. I did not realize that this flourish at the end really contradicted everything that had gone before. When Schweitzer came to Europe and his

17

picture appeared I made him one of my heroes and, with a huge cut-out of Charlie Chaplin, he hung over my bed.

Schweitzer attracted some of us whereas the teachers of religion repelled everyone. My father jestingly complained of the rabbis who scolded the people who were absent. But at least they were the cause of laughter since they were parodied. Even great rabbis like Maybaum and Baeck were targets of very funny imitations. But the younger generation of Christian teachers had lost all humour. They looked hard and made everything feel cold. The right-wing *Kreuzzeitung* identified the cross of Christ with military might, revenge, anti-Semitism, and the dread of socialism. You could not laugh at the preachers of established religion.

At this stage I learnt to distinguish between the common run of men and the élite who merely smiled at these vulgarities. I reserved my contempt for teachers and sided with the great writers. My father had a pupil in the house of the publishers S. Fischer which was within walking distance. Gerhart Hauptmann could be seen crossing the streets. The Mann brothers, Thomas and Heinrich, also turned up on rare occasions. Max Scheler and Alfred Döblin were Jews of outstanding brilliance who converted to Catholicism and salvaged the name of Jesus from his vulgar detractors. Neither of them lived out their lives in unclouded felicity within the bosom of the Catholic Church, but at the time their conversion created a stir. That Jews should find a home in this alien and hostile environment seemed incredible, but others were to follow. Franz Werfel was to become the most notable convert; his *Song of Bernadette*, though not his best novel, became a bestseller in 1941.

I gazed at these figures, when they crossed my path, with admiration. They taught me unknowingly to live in a world of one's own, free from the nastiness of fixed religious positions. Even their adherence to a church gave an air of irresponsible freedom to the stuffiness of the institution. I used the names of the famous as magical incantations — Schweitzer, Harnack, Scheler.

Berlin-Grunewald in 1928 did not force upon me any decisions. The last flowering of this liberal culture could embrace every shade of Christian feeling, agnostic moralism, and political atheism. My mother neither cared for, nor really understood, any of these forces. Suppressed as a child, passionate by nature, and driven into rebellion against bourgeois tradition, she imbibed the spirit of the twenties. She had recited Nietzsche as a child and could quote long stretches from *Thus Spake Zarathustra*. She disposed of anything that smelled of tradition, though she never surrendered her devotion to Goethe. As a result of her ambitions, confusions, and longings, she threw out much furniture, chandeliers, pottery, and clothes that reminded her of the old days. She professed to love modernity and read the books of Shaw and Wells, as they came from the press. She even began to buy shares and attempted to make money, as they did on Wall Street. Above all, she was great fun, without a shred of religious feeling. The great wide world, and success in the world, parties every night, and new occupations, such as speaking on the radio, constituted for her the good life. Yet this good life still relied on the assumption that the moral code prevailed. With all her acclamation of the new freedom she never doubted that husband and wife remain faithful to each other and that children are loved at home and return this love by loyalty. I learnt from her that curious amalgam of romantic wildness and financial awareness, a religion without dogma.

My father's influence waned under this impact of her emotional strength and practical action. He could not compete with atonal excitement or jazz, which reached us now from America. My brother had gone to London to learn the trade of journalism and he brought back with him the tunes of the first sound films. The whole world wept with and for 'Sonny Boy', danced 'Singing in the Rain' in *Forty-second Street*, and soon laughed at *The Gold Rush* and *City Lights*. The little bands of musicians in the cinemas were no longer needed. Cabarets opened in the smart districts, and my mother's friends became famous overnight as they delivered themselves of new hit numbers or cruel parodies. The city was ablaze with light and traffic. The boom spread everywhere. The mark was stable, the dollars came pouring in, and shares doubled in value. But my father made only little progress. An opera based upon a classical libretto had its first performance in

Stuttgart, but the success was short-lived, because the German President Ebert happened to have died unexpectedly following the night of the *première*. My father turned to poems by Rilke and Hölderlin and set these sad, deep, religious verses to music. But the world of the twenties showed little eagerness for the *Book of Hours* or the *Duino Elegies*. The critics respected the works, but they disdained the aristocratic, esoteric spirituality which they represent. Even Richard Strauss and Bruno Walter were deaf to his subtle otherworldliness of monastic chastity.

I had my own reasons to dislike my father's monastic spirituality. As a young child he had taken me to Kloster Neuburg where the monks had refused to admit me. The 'little girl', which was myself with long hair, must not enter the all-male establishment. Even when the mistake was now only remembered as a comic event my dislike of the cloistered spirit remained strong. I disapproved of anything soft and regarded Rilke and Hölderlin as dangerous. I came to blame them for my father's frustrations in the world. Yet the smart films and shows also contained a threat. During the last years at school I learnt that in order to survive you have to play different parts as the scenario around you changes. You have to endure your father's unsuccessful sensibility, enjoy your mother's warm sociability, profit from your brother's latest records, beat your friends at games, such as table-tennis and bridge, impress your masters with tricks, dress to be seen on Sundays, offer cigarettes to the girls, pretend to like a drink, and suffer your own masculinity, alone, exciting, and strange.

We were still children, carried away not only by every blast of doctrine but also by every new enthusiasm. There was none of the sadness of adolescence which Gide and Mauriac have so marvellously conveyed for their generation. We interpreted our history through the eyes of pleasure, and if gratification could not be obtained we withdrew happily into ourselves. I drew up a dogmatic religion for myself, whose rock bottom was myself, free from all encumbrances, indebted to none, and yet in communion with nature and destined to live for ever. Such a religion, it seemed to me, could make sense of this strange world, as long as I could transform it through my own fantasies. There was then no veto on these fantasies in which the hero suffered and triumphed. This heroic self constantly interpreted the world around one. The enticing images within provided a kind of documentary film against the boredom of history. Yet one also sensed that perhaps, at the bottom of it all, there yawned a void and that one might be sucked or trapped into it. Pleasure and fear equipped the rising generation for the coming battles. The main thing was to float above the void and to let the fear be kept at bay by pleasures. The question 'What is Christianity?' ceased to matter and old Harnack could go to sleep. We had better fish to fry.

3

THE DECLINE OF THE WEST

Sickness answers to the needs of the spirit, and I ended this period of atomic existence in the molecular whirlpool with a patch on the lung. The hot sunshine and the cold water of the Lago Maggiore achieved the physical discomfiture which my soul sensed in that golden Paradise at the end of the twenties. In the fishing village of Ascona artists worked, entertained, and suffered. We spent a season among them, and the world opened perspectives of corruption to which the adolescent fantasy responded with eagerness. It was hot. The lake shimmered in blue, enfolded by the hills. Flowers and fruit on trellises abounded, hung over the fences, crept up the hillsides. The church bells rang the Angelus. I could dream, swim, dive, and fall in love. There were beautiful boys, naked like statues. There were girls, concealed and distant. And there were the mountains above, the still nights, the silent piazzas in the early morning, the wine, and always the sun. Then news came of my grandfather's death. My parents quarrelled. My brother refused to live at home. I spat blood, did not return to school, but, exiled by the North Sea, in gales and under grey skies, I had to lie for hours. Medical checks registered satisfactory progress: I regained weight, the roughness mellowed, I could go home.

My universe had been penetrated by the X-ray treatment and dissolved into shadows. First I had tasted of beauty unutterable, which needed no prayers, nor angels, nor sermons. Then I had seen nothing at all, except the surgeries, white coats, uniformed nurses, silent doctors, institutional cold shoulders. Trains, boats, faces, arrivals, departures spun the web of a neutral world. The world was a great hotel and you had to pay the bill.

I learnt then that the greatest enemy is boredom. I still had to lie on my back at home, and I entered the circle of the void. Friends called and bored me. My brother wrote from

London, my father looked in, my mother sat by my bed. One talked of school, of how to make up for lost time, of meals, sport, and the yawn of the world widened. The picture of God had now faded into nothing. I decided to get well, to strip off all the nonsense of childhood, to be like the others. My best friend never had trouble with gods, ran faster than any of his age, received prizes, and climbed the ladder. The maid in his house became pregnant; the thing, then a serious crime, was hushed up and the abortion performed. He neither boasted nor regretted anything. The moral universe never existed at all. We had been fooled with the categorical imperative and the Kantian call to duty. Instead we began to play with more fashionable ideas.

Oswald Spengler (1880-1936) popularized an historical fatalism which appealed to the large class of disenchanted idealists. *The Decline of the West* became a cliché which covered the whole series of sad decays of cultures and high organisms. Spengler talked in pretentious terms of a 'morphology' of world-history. From China to the West we count the ruins and build museums for them. Every species seems to go through the same stages of development and fulfil the pattern of ascent and descent. The stage which we call civilization is by no means the peak, but marks the falling-off towards the final eclipse. Only a superficial judgement can exempt Christianity from this cycle, for Christendom is in reality not one religion but a continuum into which contrasting cultures have issued. The Christian religion lent an aura of illusion to cultures in their pre-scientific stage. The mythical wrapping-up of reality, however, fails now, as it has failed in the past. Even without the war the shape of the West had to obey the dictates of dissolution. Spengler fed unwittingly the radicalism of those who did not wish to submit to total pessimism. Either they could turn left, and acclaim the rise of Russia as the future power; or they could, with the fanatics of the right, fight for the 'new order'. Surprisingly, Spengler himself did not fare well with the Nazis; after a brief honeymoon period he was out of favour, since he could not be fooled by them; true rejuvenation was impossible.

Spengler was explosive stuff. We walked to and fro, endlessly discussing determinism and freewill. Good though it was to be rid of 'blind obedience' I had a sneaking feeling of disquiet. If a sense of duty was not so much a virtue as a deception then we had no 'starry sky' above use, nor the voice of conscience within us. If these twin pillars collapsed, I asked, how could we live? Could I violate my cousin whom I loved, or lie with my friend's sister whom I did not care for? No, replied my friend. We were in the world to get our qualifications and earn our keep, not like his own father who had fallen on the last day of the war, but in some sensible profession. The prospects were bright. Sport pointed the way. One could always improve one's speed, or the length or height of the jump, or the throw of the discus.

I fixed a punch ball in my room. I must become a boxer like Max Schmeling. I ran in the woods. I ignored the full moon and all the poems to the moon. I avoided the family. I practised autonomy: be oneself and raise no further questions. I worked hard at mathematics, for this science made no demands on one's feelings. I tried to reduce all things to numbers. The true religion was the Number One, the total Unity, remote, oneself. Alas, the boredom remained, only slightly mitigated by table-tennis.

Then, unexpectedly and out of the blue, came an illumination. In order to matriculate (the *Abitur*) we had to 'do' a bit of Plato. I fingered the leaves of the German translation and suddenly I was transfixed with a new vision of life. Books had never meant a great deal to me. Even then comic strips had begun to destroy the world of letters. Plato had no balloons coming out of funny mouths. Plato reported what Socrates had taught, how he had argued, and how he had stood his trial and met his fate. Plato lifted me out of the sickly emotionalism and its boredom which had sterilized my mind. The cool dialectic gripped me. I even looked up words I did not know. I identified myself with the man in the cave who had not realized that he was groping uselessly in darkness. Plato bade me come out and see a universe which was not primarily concerned with me, my fears, and the shattered warmth of childhood. Nor did Plato preach blind obedience and engage in uncritical demands. Plato was my guide in the confident taking stock of things as they were. We were, after all, immortal. Our souls were independent of the body. Ideas reigned and matter conformed. The universe was good, true, and beautiful, and its spirit was available to us. Socrates was inspired and trusted the good demon which prevented him from dishonourable actions, flight, or cowardice. He could look forward to death, not through self-pity nor in a spirit of revenge, but because either painless sleep or happy communion awaited him.

I was amazed that no one had ever mentioned Plato to me before. The generation of my parents knew of Plato but only gave me a superior smile when I contributed his doctrines to their concerns. My father was an exception and reacted to my enthusiasm with his own harmonies, knowing that I was ready for the world of music. He had given us tickets for the opera before, and I had also been to his own recitals. But now he took me to the Bach Festival, and the four cantatas I then heard began another chapter of life. I did not go unprepared. I was sufficiently advanced in the playing of the violin to understand something of musical structure, and my father brought heavy volumes of Bach's works from the State Library so that we could see the score. He always insisted that the orchestral score must be seen and not only heard.

It so happened that the four cantatas embraced the whole of life: *'Es ist dir gesagt, Mensch, was gut ist'* (ethics), *'Sie werden aus Saba alle kommen'* (Christ), *'Watchet auf'* (human response), and *'Nun ist das Heil und die Kraft'* (worship and adoration). Moreover, the audience added a flavour of celestial-human solidarity, such as I had never experienced in church or at school. Unaware of their own social labels — rich or poor, workers and lawyers, nurses and doctors, pious and agnostics, Jews and Gentiles — they seemed to be united as they were absorbed, like sleepers roused by the virgins' call to the wedding.

The spiritual transport exceeded my powers of explanation. I was on fire to know, not only why I enjoyed this music as if it were a miracle, but also how it related to mathematics, and thence to our minds. I was bound to ask if the Christian texts were incidental or central to the composer's art. But my father remained quite unapproachable, following his own thoughts with a snorting sound, which informed the world that he was absent. The conductor of the bus came round for the fare, but it was left to me to pay. Later when we attended the Passion my father even dwelt on the text according to Matthew and John, the difference of treatment, not only in the music but also in the Gospels, but he remained non-committal as to the faith in both. In a way, the music was the faith, and Bach was the mediator of God. Only when he no longer lived with me, did he connect Bach with the great theologians and the architecture of truth, as handed down in the *Summa Theologiae* of St Thomas Aquinas. Bach's *Art of Fugue*, I learnt much later, patterns the inexhaustible contradictions of faith in a vast arc of fugal harmony. I am consoled that my father faced his death at Auschwitz with Bach's 'When we are in greatest need' and 'Herewith I stand before the throne of God' and thus offered death to life, in the eternal counterpoint.

Neither public events nor private decisions, however, were then shaped by Platonic idealism and Bach's polyphony. The last years at school were without soul. Yet they yielded one further discovery which was to be even more influential in my life than any other. Our set book in English was *Macbeth*, and soon I knew the whole play by heart. Shakespeare spoke to my enforced aloofness. Macbeth became my hero. Macbeth also threatened me. Shakespeare elevated the great amoralist, the murderer with a heroic imagination, the husband whose weakness is exposed by his lady, and even the Scottish mists penetrated my desires, ambitions, and dread. But the relentless sequence of more blood, the hard joyless triumph, and the final defeat disclosed to me the 'idiot's delight' I had been planning for myself in my proud self-isolation. I did not want to end up as a poor player, strutting and fretting upon the stage, with perhaps a crazed wife who cannot rub out the dark stain of common guilt.

Macbeth achieved for me at my most disturbed state a faith which acknowledged the reality of demonic temptation, of murder, treachery, and despair. Shakespeare had formalized, without taming, the wild savagery of hell. Just as I had once moved in heaven with the Homeric gods, in games of war and banquets, feeding on ambrosia and drinking nectar, so now I could descend to hell and face the ghosts of the slain.

Unconsciously our generation prepared for the 'huddling together of fierce extremes, a war of opposite natures' (Hazlitt), which in *Macbeth* sickens our souls with its sudden, startling, violent transitions from light to shade. One wanted to be Macbeth, one feared Macbeth, one longed to get rid of Macbeth. Shakespeare began for me a revelation which was never to end. It was paired with Dostoyevsky's *Crime and Punishment*. The murderer Raskolnikov, unlike Macbeth, never attracted me. I found him pitiable and loathsome, just as Dostoyevsky had intended him to be, and as the real prototype probably had been. This would-be Napoleon, who kills the old usurer, and, through an unfortunate but typical complication, also her sister, discredited the little faith I still had in self-isolation.

Crime and Punishment also revealed an unsuspected item which hitherto I had failed to register. Raskolnikov, I now saw, was himself a victim of his environment. He was conditioned to be a criminal, without witches to whisper to him. His guilt preceded his crime, and not the other way round as I had always imagined. His fantasies induced in him the need to fulfil the killing he had so often pictured. After the murder he hardly bothered to retrieve and use the stolen money. To crown the sequence of events, he sought, almost in spite of himself, peace through confession. He lacked contrition and only Sonya could by degrees evoke in him the stronger response of penitence.

I imbibed the vocabulary of atonement. Raskolnikov's slow and sulky resurrection, even after Sonya's reading of the *Raising of Lazarus*, gave me more hope of redemption than any sudden conversion would have done. I wondered what would happen at the end in the penal settlement in Siberia. This Russian Christ had nothing in common with my nurse's piety, nor the Church's cult, nor Harnack's essence of Christianity. A young pastor, a brilliant lawyer who had left the courts for the pulpit, shared my enthusiasm: 'You must read Dostoyevsky's other works, especially *The Brothers Karamazov*'. I did not want a book-list but pinpointed the problem of the criminal's restoration. Could a murderer serve his sentence and start afresh? Could he be forgiven? He criticized my approach: 'You are being too literal. A novelist personalizes universal issues. Otherwise he could not sell his novels. But in reality we are concerned with society and social issues. All moral questions deal with society.'

He evaded my question by enlarging on Christian socialism, the only hope in the future. He mentioned a string of names and slogans, the Blumhardts, Ragaz, the American Rauschenbusch, a certain Englishman, F.D. Maurice. 'Jesus is Victor' because Lazarus was being raised in our whole degraded, exploited, and exploiting society. Tolstoy had shown the way. Had I heard of Paul Tillich, his teacher? Yes, Christian socialism could open the door of the tomb.

The enumeration of famous names, which I had never heard of, left me cold. Instead, the social colossus found its own way of laying its hand upon me. The cause of two American Italians, called Sacco and Vanzetti, stirred the public in 1926. These men were under sentence of death, and some of the finest European spirits, such as Romain Rolland, Anatole France, Masaryk, Einstein, led a crusade in their support. They firmly asserted that these working-class anarchists were innocent of the crimes with which they were charged and for which they were about to be martyred by a cruel and unjust class of oppressors. Sacco, a shoe factory hand, and Vanzetti, a fish pedlar, had come to America in 1908 and were known to be 'subversive'. When, on 15 April 1920, a paymaster and guard of a shoe factory in South Braintree, Mass., were killed and robbed of $16,000 these 'Reds' were duly arrested. The trial in 1921 followed a wave of anti-radicalism, and although no proper evidence was submitted, the court found the accused guilty on 14 July. An appeal was refused, but the convicted murderers were still alive in 1926 and the case had received a renewed publicity since another gang seemed to be identified through a confession offered in 1925. Worldwide protests were organized, but their 'leftist' sympathies only served to alienate the Puritan and Catholic united front in Massachusetts against the 'apostates' and their interfering friends outside.

The niceties of the case did not concern us as we marched in huge columns, which converged upon the Wittenbergplatz. The bands led the masses, which obeyed a kind of military precision, inherited from former days. The blood-red and the republican black-red-and-gold flags preceded the banners which demanded justice for the condemned men and the punishment of their judges. We sang revolutionary hymns, incantations of freedom, the sun, the dawn of a better world. We were bound in a brotherhood of which The Internationale, repeated often, was creed and ritual. I fused my youth and enthusiasm with the bitter resentment of wrinkled old men. At last I experienced liberation from self. Here, unknown to me, was the heady toxic brew of ecstasy, as only groups, united in protests, can produce and induce. The wave of solidarity drowned all reservations. How could anyone doubt the sacred cause? Sacco and Vanzetti, held high on banners (I thought, for but a moment, that Sacco looked terribly funny), were already saints who spearheaded the kingdom of the future, and I had found with and in those hundreds of thousands the faith and the sacrament of socialist salvation. I could put a lid on all former hopes and fears. I could end reflection. From now on we, the great brotherhood, were God.

Sacco and Vanzetti, still protesting their innocence, were executed on 23 August 1927. A committee of distinguished lawyers upheld the death sentence as the result of a fair trial.

4

HAMMER, SICKLE, AND SWASTIKA

The Wall Street crash and the ensuing worldwide crisis have been described and analysed in countless books. Even pictures adumbrate the spectacular impact. The chimneys of the factories no longer smoked, the workers were unemployed, the bankrupts committed suicide, and the leaders conferred. But the spiritual consequences were and remained hidden to the world. There were no Ezekiels who boldly articulated the Lord's will for famine, pestilence, and exile, as a punishment for apostasy. Yet the secular writers of the time at least parodied the judgement, and while the depression escalated — my mother quite mistakenly gloried in the low prices, deflation having brought a fine goose down to less than one pound — one read and discussed Wells, Galsworthy, Upton Sinclair, and other social critics forgotten now. Thomas Mann's *The Magic Mountain* had appeared and the 'magician' received the Nobel Prize. This long chronicle of voluntary disease concerned the period before the First World War, but its mocking humour extended to our feverish indulgence in sickness. The tubercles of the anti-hero Hans Castorp, the ordinary man, and his companions, now ran riot in our world. *The Magic Mountain* explicated a potent theology of death. We were the *moribundi*: doctors, idealists, moralists, drug-takers, profiteers, nationalists, materialists, Jesuits, and Jews. Even beautiful women sentenced themselves to death with trivial self-gratification in a parasitical society which ate itself into the grave. Despite its lust it had no life. The beautiful boys and girls were as rotten as their sick lungs. The immense surgeon, Hofrat Behrens called Rhadamantys king of the underworld, presided over his empire. The brave were too stupid to recover, the clever too weak to live, and the dead were hidden from the survivors, as their corpses were carried unobserved on toboggans into the valley for burial. Mann's exposure of nihilistic capitalism ended on the little man's disappearance under the shrapnel of the battlefields of the Western Front. 'Could anyone ever again love?' remained the final question, even after the war and now after the depression. The millionaires finished jumping out of the windows before long, but I realized that my childhood's confidence had been misplaced.

Yet Thomas Mann also helped me out of my cynicism. In his novel he exempted one class from the sentence of death through boredom and corruption. The local working people, woodcutters above Davos, were unaffected. The working class was the god who must save. Everyone on the left came to worship the star which had risen in the east. Hammer and sickle were free from the decadent past. We, who were neither workers nor peasants, must offer ourselves to the party of Marx, Lenin, and Stalin.

I abandoned the mood of free inquiry. I wanted dogma. I tried to read Marx's *Das Kapital* and trampled on my mood of boredom while I persisted in turning the pages. I also proved my new faith by buying the Communist newspapers. I learnt the jargon from the *Rote Fahne* (which was sometimes proscribed and then appeared with an aura of greater glory). But of all my reading of propaganda I retain nothing except a lasting allergy. Only the cutting story of *The Good Soldier Schweyk* influenced me with a continuing dread of clericalism, for this clever tale of a Czech 'soldier', who is a mixture of Falstaff and Sancho Panza, really succeeded in defrocking the sacred ministry. Schweyk serves a number of priests who excel in gambling, cheating, drinking, and fornicating. The author uses the light touch of comedy to make his work a classic of popular atheism. The shoddy priests stand for an absurd Jesus who reveals the monumental idiocy and profitability of religion. Schweyk became my spiritual godfather as I entered the movement, rather than Walter Ulbricht, the party-boss who was dull and disliked by all. With a worker's cap on one's head, a red tie on a blue shirt, we sold illegal papers at factory gates, painted slogans ('Freedom and Bread', to my mother's great amusement) and met in the beer-cellars of the proletariat.

Religion had been harmless, but ideology created risks. The inititation into the party brought great advantages: one could at last vanquish self-isolation. But the solidarity had to be paid for by total assent. It was no longer called 'blind obedience', but survival without a willingness to incur danger was unthinkable. The nightly forays with paint were an exciting training ground. But greater sacrifices came along, though they were never spelt out openly. Some comrades were armed; I had the courage to resist, and I did not even listen to such exploits as minor robberies and shoot-outs with the Nazis. On the other hand I was fool enough to lend my parents' home for a cover address. Letters arrived from abroad and had to be forwarded to other addresses given inside the first envelope. Was I playing with fire, or not? Once I opened the missive and was reassured by the innocent nature of the enclosure. I knew nothing yet of coded messages. Credulity is not a religious preserve, and an unquestioned ideology fosters a naive trust. Moscow was our Mecca, and Stalin the only prophet.

I never encountered any interest in religion among our comrades. The party line demanded godlessness, and with this virtue we complied gladly. But anti-church propaganda was too dull and irrelevant to be popular. Once we gathered round a Salvation Army group with threats and abuse. They ceased singing and disbanded, but I was struck by a pair of eyes which suffered acceptance in a way that haunted me.

Under the surface of tough behaviour I was still compounded of discretion, fear, and a feeling of providential election. When the comrades arranged a provocative demonstration in front of the army barracks and when the angry soldiers, reacting to our 'Bread and Freedom' cries, came out, with swords and fixed bayonets, smartly dealing out blows and evidently enjoying the chase of the running Reds, I stood quite still and the tide passed me by. I neither ran, nor hid, but, strangely confident, looked up to the stars and felt protected. A year later, in 1930 before the elections which brought the Nazis into menacing prominence, at Worms, I again stood my ground in aboslute tranquility. The women had mistaken my wind-jacket for a para-Nazi uniform and suddenly their men came forward to lynch me. My school friends saw the oncoming assualt but did nothing to defend me. Hands gripped me and ferocious

32

eyes stared at me. Above all the shouting I prayed inwardly for protection and just looked at my enemies. The attack flagged and then stopped altogether. The boys welcomed me back, laughing to cover their shame. But I thought, how Luther's 'Here I stand' had repeated itself in the same Worms where he had appeared in 1521. I also reflected how clothes make the man, and how we expose ourselves to false judgements. I had been taken for a Nazi.

Could I ever have become a Nazi, if my race had not excluded me from the start? Could I have joined the S.A. or the S.S., marched under the blood-red flag with the swastika? Could I have been touched by this new ideology, which reverted to a religion of blood and soil? This religion, which now spread like wildfire, sprouted in the misery of millions and flourished by the disenchantment of the victims of war and inflation. Revenge, law, order, work, cleanliness, land, and even God were promised. Strength was to be obtained by joy. The home was to be restored. The streets were to be freed, and the new heroic community be formed in solidarity with all the martyred heroes. Germany would wake up, Judah perish. March, march, march! Brown and black. I witnessed their companies, changing trains at Gleisdreieck station, giants with death's-head insignias on their caps. They savoured violence, victory, torture, death. I saw the Apocalypse of our age.

'For the last time', they sang. The trumpet called. Now was the time of salvation. The Day was not far off. Shopkeepers, assistants, lawyers, accountants, officials, directors, hailed the man who could restore the solid old order and also end the present, the non-man (*Unmensch*, as Thomas Mann called him) who drew into himself all the empty resentments.

He was the Antichrist, nihilist, insane, powerful, seductive. He mixed truths with lies. He foretold his actions and warned his future victims, but he did not release them out of his clutches. He had the eyes of the basilisk and spread an aura of demonic divinity. He remembered everything. He had an intuitive understanding of men. He attracted the good to suck it dry. Mothers, maidens, babies, fathers, boys, toddlers, could be enfolded in his vast sentimental sweep. Men of the Christian faith looked to him. He was destined by God, providence had selected him, he personified the people, mediated the mystery of life. He spoke and they followed.

But this *dance macabre* rallied also beery burghers, the widows of fallen officers, the haughty bankers, the rational thinkers, scientists, and artists. It was an Apocalypse of bourgeois stickiness; the cynics disguised themselves as enthusiasts. The machine ran on secret funds rather than cosmic energy. Yet it nearly foundered in 1932 when the sensational successes at the elections ended. It almost seemed that reason and morality would prevail over mass hysteria. But Antichrist, like a sleepwalker, walked to his throne. A final plot,[1] the crop of many deceptions, lifted the gangster Lucifer into the seat of tyranny.

Throughout these years I marvelled at the collapse of faiths, convictions, loyalties. Where was now the power of the new psychology? Could Freud and Adler confront the black armour? Where did Einstein's relativity begin to bite in a sea of waving arms? How could Planck assert quantum physics in this predestined rush of molecules? Why did not the poems, sketches, novels of liberal writers sweep away the oozing drip of lies? Was there no spiritual power, no firm fortress, not even a prayer left?

The final blow came when the Communists made common cause with the Nazis in 1932. This was Stalin's masterstroke, repeated later with even more irony in 1939, when Ribbentrop and Molotov signed the agreement which carved up Poland. All the claptrap of dialectical materialism, endlessly discussed in salons, culminated now in the final twist of the rapier of treachery. The dark forces were in command and opened the abyss for well-meaning, naive socialists, pacifists, progressive intellectuals. But the state of trance continued. The Inferno includes not only traitors but also the wilfully betrayed. Spiritual fraud triumphed on 30 January 1933, and when the Reichstag burnt a few weeks later it flared like a torch of doom. The gloating faces of the victors shone in candle-light as they processed. Darkness had become light, usurped the light.

[1] The ageing and reluctant President Hindenburg was the dupe of his own son, on the verge of bankruptcy and useful as go-between.

The faith in Antichrist is too complex to be deciphered in simple terms. The mixture of materialistic selfishness and romantic idealism cannot account for the sadistic streak, nor can the loss of the individual in the mass explain the personal pride of each follower. His willingness to give his life proves his sincerity. I then began to learn the bitter lesson that sincerity is no guide to goodness and truth.

My father dismissed these developments since they were political and he had no interest in politics. My mother, already in deep trouble with the police over some share transactions (honest but rendered illegal through some emergency law), decided the time had come to disband and to flee abroad. She was alone in her unruffled foresight. Among our friends business continued, as far as possible, as usual. Some even pinned their hopes on tighter discipline. Others declared that the new regime could never last. The Communists welcomed it as a stepping-stone in the right direction (they were proved right in the long run). But the most typical reaction to Antichrist missed its whole religious mode and indulged in shrugging off the childish excesses from the legitimate and serious purpose of remaking the nation and ending unemployment.

I reacted differently, because I looked at the faces in power. The eyes, noses, lips, hair of all the devils spoke to me as Satan, Beliar, Beelzebub effected portraits in the mind of Milton. I withdrew into my cold solitude to cover up my tracks and remove all marks of my identity. One false move would lead to protective custody, which I had once believed, in good faith, to protect the prisoner from the mob. I had learnt just in time. I now made a pact with God, like Jacob, whose story I read in this dire plight. Given shelter, food, and clothes and an open road, I would in return acknowledge the beneficent power as my Lord. Biding my time with precision, I packed a minimum of belongings into one suitcase, enclosed a sum of money, which, if found, would wreck my chance of escape. 'Fear not', said the Scriptures, to which I now resorted, and I approached the Dutch frontier station calmly. Even as the customs official, escorted and supervised by a black guard, checked the luggage, opened the case, and put his hands on my treasure, so that I could hear the crinkling of the bank-notes, I prayed and felt no alarm. His attention wandered, the black guard nodded, handed me my passport, and soon the train moved on. I crossed the English Channel on April Fools' Day 1933.

5

THIS PRECIOUS ISLE

Though still depressed economically and politically isolated England was to the refugee a green and pleasant land. He was not allowed to work nor be a burden on the community. Despite this contradiction he could obtain a permit of residence which was renewable. At the police station in Bow Street, London, he could suffer humiliation. The Home Office could and did refuse extensions or papers of re-entry. The alien was never directly told how unwelcome he was, but he had to be very thick-skinned if he believed in a future in the British Isles. The organizations were either unhelpful or openly advocating emigration to other countries. But these other countries made it equally clear that they desired no influx from this source. Palestine looked like Paradise on many horizons, but the quota system reduced the hoped-for stream to a thin trickle. The corridors of agencies, consulates, information centres, over-flowed with the wreckage of Jewish lawyers, doctors, business-men, intellectuals, and tailors. Their wives and children hum-med in the background, a diapason of pain and the assertion of the right to live. In 1933 the flood could still be directed, out of London, to distant parts. The suitcases became the sym-bol of the uprooted.

We aliens were in a goodly company, with Ruth among the alien corn and with Virgil 'aliens in a land unknown'. But we did not enjoy the pathos. Alienation is a compound of frustra-tion and anxiety. Without money, friends, and too much time on his hands, the alien waits for a direct outcome of his trou-bles. The interpretation of his state he leaves to others, such as Kierkegaard and Kafka. Yet their experience of inner homeless-ness had prefigured the enforced estrangement from outside. These anonymous thousands, who in the thirties were little more than a harbinger of the flood to come, acted out the dra-ma of alienation in search of de-alienation and taking root. With amazing insight Kafka, for example, had already patterned the kind of salvation the outcast would seek.

The most common desire was emigration to America. Just as in Kafka's *Amerika* Karl arrives from Germany, which he had to leave on some vague charge, and in New York enters into a comic network of confidence tricksters and Utopian engagements, so the refugee from Europe attempted to solve his state of 'unwanted' by getting affidavit, visa, and ticket to the promised land. Only a few managed it, for the quota restrictions were strict and by no means lifted by the Roosevelt administration. They were the lucky ones who profited from, and gave a new impetus to, the powerful religion of the New World, the asylum of the rejected, the land of the free, America.

I also obtained an affidavit and was ready to apply for my visa, when I discovered another way of salvation, namely, that of staying in England by free choice and love. As in Kafka's stories of *The Great Wall of China* and *The Burrow*, I looked for safety and acceptance where I was. I trusted the fortifications of English life, and England was then a kind of burrow, still separate from the Continent, never yet invaded for centuries, and incredibly stable. True, unemployment and the crisis had created the common miseries, but in London, Oxford, and Cambridge the structure remained strong. The King and the Queen drove through the City in an open carriage. The dead were honoured in two minutes' silence throughout the country on 11 November. Even the grey fog added to the impenetrable density of English life. Laughter and parody did not undermine this insular unity, and even the discomforts of bad sanitary arrangements, inadequate heating, cold and drafty rooms, watery cooking, confirmed the stranger in his mistaken confidence that here he could be accepted and safe. But his mistake rested really upon the unspoken, unidentified, unquestioned norms of morality in the island. Here was 'fair play', not exceedingly generous and certainly not hospitable, but enabling the little strange animal to find a burrow. Unlike Kafka's animal, the refugee, if allowed to get behind the Chinese wall of the Channel, could 'live within at peace', undisturbed by interlopers and suspect noises.

The English way of life was overpowering and attractive

to those who had the good fortune to experience its full spectrum. It was almost as if Shakespeare's plays were being re-enacted for us, so as to naturalize us spiritually. England without Shakespeare was then, and still is, unthinkable, but for the alienated outsider Shakespeare is a passport to good fortune. I saw as many of the plays as I could, cheaply at the Old Vic, on wooden benches. Theatre, people, language, acting, even refreshments reflected, interpreted, and harmonized with the genius who could never fail to whisper, question and answer, indict and proclaim, our state in the world. Hence the England of Shakespeare could redeem the hopeless, stuck in the guilty fantasies of Macbeth, Hamlet, Lear, and Othello. Above all, I remember the experience of seeing the *Tempest*: well-prepared, as always, by a dear friend who, one of the first women to obtain a degree at Cambridge, had taken me through the text verse by verse. I did not think that our un-man could be compared to Caliban, nor that Prospero and the enchanted isle would emerge quite as unscathed in our day. But here, for the first time, I saw how the theme of reconciliation and resignation can take the lead over practical and economic business. Shakespeare remained my guide as I found a foothold in the City and worked over some boring order books. Shakespeare was England and is England, with all its contradictions.

In Christian England of the thirties an alien, frightened Perditus or Perdita, could find a home in which Shakespeare mattered more than tough mutton and drafty rooms. The natives of this island would have been surprised to know that their tolerance, indifference, and even friendliness, could be transposed by their speech, the tongue of Shakespeare, into something like a religion. The services of the Church of England were unique for the foreigner, for they derived from the sixteenth century. The Prayer Book and the Authorized Version of the Bible, though not by Shakespeare, belonged to his world. They were not touched by Protestant and Catholic antagonism. Instead they were protected by, and supported, the Crown. Here was a religion which took the class structure for granted. The hierarchical system pertained not only to the clerical orders but included churchwardens, squires, ladies and gentlemen. Though the main support for the Church came from the middle-class suburbs, the light and shadow of aristocratic patronage hovered above the ordinary routine. The Church was silent, august, awe-inspiring, and hence the divisiveness of class yielded to a sense of unity. The fragmentation of the earthly seemed as if patterned into a higher cohesion. Thus the very practical, direct and immanent outlook of the local church shared in a transcendent, cosmic order. But this partaking was not consciously striven for, nor the result of mystical endeavour. Rather the Church had inherited a tradition of life and practice which happened to have its head in heaven and its feet on earth.

The outsider could not help marvelling at this achievement which was so effortlessly accomplished. The English reserves were so strong that the Church could assume a stance of authority and superiority which could not be questioned. Local parochial strife added a spice of Shakespearean life to a dangerously respectable institution. Controversies between High and Low Church engaged the minds which loved to defend principles. But the outsider continued marvelling that this Church was conservative without being nationalistic, English without being against other races, Christian without being anti-Jewish, hierarchical without being opposed to reform, rich without cursing socialism. The Christian presence could be felt, but no one was forced to submit to force. Voluntarism governed the system, and endless societies, clubs, and organizations catered for the needs of special groups.

The English Church had withstood many attacks in the past without running for help in obscurantism. The challenges of the Puritans, Wesleyans, levellers of all sorts, evolutionists after Darwin, mockers like Shaw, critics like Wells, had brought a gain to its spiritual capital. Even defections, such as Newman's, had helped to stabilize the ship of faith. The Bible, the Prayer Book, buildings, institutions, ordained ministers, and, above all, countless lives and examples had cemented a fabric, both demanding and rewarding.

Cracks were, however, visible even to the outsider. This was not a Church to which the working class owed allegiance, beyond accepting from it the *rites de passage*, baptism, marriage, and funerals. The unions sided with the Noncomformists and their 'conscience' was held in high esteem even in church

40

circles. The Church laboured among the poor, opened missions in dark corners, and even started ambitious housing s schemes for the underprivileged. Nevertheless, despite an o overt attempt to reach the masses, the response, except in certain northern areas, remained disappointing. Even the late arrival of ordained priests of working-class origin did not change the bleak scene in the large areas of London, where only a certain amount of bribery, such as the promise of clothing or an outing, could induce the parents to send their children to Sunday-school. This element of bribery was also not altogether absent from the home missions to minorities, such as the Jews. Advantages could still be gained by 'Rice Christians', in England as well as in India.

Another less noticeable weakness was the long-standing apostasy on the part of the rich. Many titled personages were patrons of church livings, but had long ago given up the Christian faith. Their preference for self-gratification, by way of the newly invented machines, swamped their moral sense. This apostasy received a sensational focus in King Edward VIII's determination to marry a Mrs Simpson, an American divorcée.

These critical confrontations between Church and State were still far off as I came to join the Church of England. Honeysuckle and ancient towers, tombs and silken gowns, green swards and boys and girls, fill the mental picture, over which preside benign priests in starched white surplices over black cassocks. The sanctuary was central. There were the holy shrine, the burning candles, the aumbry, a processional cross, servers making ready the altar. The bell rang for early service and the congregation, scarcely nodding and never talking, filled the pews, kneeled down, and listened, prayed, replied in hushed voices to the 'Lift up your Hearts', and embodied in their silent posture the *Sanctus,* looking towards the east, yet entirely without ecstasy, but controlled within the comprehensive unity of the one cosmos, the one Church, one nation and people. They received the consecrated Bread and Wine with devotion, returned to their pews, bowed for the blessing, stayed on their knees, until the priest and servers departed and the candles were extinguished. On reaching the porch a few greetings would be exchanged, within an air of

41

expressed goodwill, and even the stranger departed, though unknown, as if comprehended by the community.

The later services struck me as more problematic. To begin with, the music was on the whole infernal. Though in cathedrals the boys' voices rose with crystal purity to the sky and the organ thundered, the repertoire even there was poor, stained by Victorian sentimentality, which marked 'trouble' with *piano* and 'death' with *pianissimo*. The chants repeated banal phrases over and over again, and the hymns with a few exceptions added treacly slush to words of egregious idiocy. To one brought up on Bach these strange survivals of a religion, which discredited itself in every line and melody, never ceased to be repugnant. However, there were cases of good taste, especially in Anglo-Catholic churches where the Masses of Haydn, Mozart, and Schubert could often be heard. But they were eclectic and not typical.

However, far more serious was the theological torpor of the sermons. Whereas the Prayer Book seemed to commit the Church to some very strong declarations on grace and election, some of which sounded as if they came from Calvin's Geneva, the preachers seemed to have no very clear ideas on anything. Unknown to them, most of them wallowed in the shallow waters of liberal ethics. They seemed to be unaware of the Christian heritage and often merely paraphrased the readings. Here again the Anglo-Catholics stood out with a rigorous programme of ascetic ideals, sacramental practice, and a Church-centred doctrine of salvation which echoed the ancient exclusivism. They did, however, not preach, but only taught. True preaching, of the biblical and missionary kind, could be heard at lunchtime services in the City of London, where the workers flocked to hear the prophetic voice. What it left out, however, was more marked than what it articulated: the voice uttered no alarm and ignored the gathering clouds of conflict.

The English Church of all shades accepted peace as its central message in answer to the moral crisis threatening the world. Though Union Jacks stood in the sanctuaries and colour parades were a regular feature, the search for peace fuelled the energies of the Christian consciousness. One did not have to belong to the Peace Pledge Union nor gather round

Dick Sheppard, a much loved Anglican pacifist, who blended in typically English fashion the doctrine of non-violence as handed down by Tolstoy, Schweitzer, and Gandhi. Everybody prayed for 'no more war', and the famous resolution 'not to fight for King and Country' by the students at Oxford, which was to have such a disastrous effect upon events, merely echoed Christian feeling. Protestants and Catholics were not divided in their suspicion of anti-German propaganda. Lord Halifax typified the Anglo-Catholic temperament which not only prayed for peace but also wished to appease in the belief that the blessed peacemakers can bring about a change for the better. My Protestant pastor, who rose at dawn to pray, also deplored with penitence the treatment Germany had received by the treaty of Versailles. The biblical word 're-conciliation' fed the earnest desire to bury the hatred left over from the war. Hence Churchill's warnings were denounced as mischievous propaganda, and the policy of the editor of *The Times* confirmed English Christians in the belief that when certain just demands were met mankind — which was then Europe — could look forward to peace and progress. Even the Labour Party endorsed this pledge for peace and favoured disarmament. *Dona nobis pacem* covered the ground.

The passion for peace was the common denominator for a variety of motives. Some Christians simply desired a quiet life (as authorized by the Prayer of Intercession) and the maintenance of the *status quo*; others abhorred violence in any form, claiming that war never paid and was always the greater evil; a few sided with Fascism, Nazism, and reactionary forces in society, in the name of the Christian tradition. However, the religious ideal went further than that, for the ecumenical goal had already been set. Peace was nothing but a first step towards unity in Christ, and therefore the inspired leaders of many branches of Christendom organized for the reunion of Christendom. 'Pax' became, therefore, internationally the slogan for a renewed Christian brotherhood. What was called the 'scandal of our divisions' was to be done away with, and an almost utopian conviction guided bishops, prelates, and presidents towards a consummation of this grand scheme of unity within our lifetime.

Clearly, this outlook was the reverse of 1914 and the German theologians' slogan 'God with us'. While the German forces rearmed feverishly, and while Russian purges went on unheeded, Western Christendom allowed itself the luxury of a happy dream. But the dream was reality in England at the time when Baldwin dared not tell the truth to the people.

In 1933 I fell ill and was rescued from death by an organization called Toc H. One of their members had heard of my plight as a student of theology, abandoned in rooms in East London. Toc H came for me and welcomed me as the child of a former enemy. This band of brothers acted in remembrance of their fallen comrades, who had in the hell of Flanders found some peace and comfort at Talbot House at a village called Poperinghe. The survivors, who also attracted the generation who had not seen war, lit a light of remembrance before their meetings. This symbolic rite, marked by silence in the dark, culminated in the recitation of the text: 'Let your light so shine before men that they may see your good works and glorify your Father'. This mystical ceremony flourished in a happy and classless society which identified the social gospel with 'paying the rent on earth'. Women served side by side with former soldiers in endless activities of aid and support. No one worried about the emphasis on good works, for they solved the immemorial problem of grace not by contrasting it with works but by implementing it with schemes of help, and in their care I learnt the lesson, which men find so difficult to learn, that to receive a gift is as much an act of grace as to give.

Toc H had international ramifications which still reflected the British Empire. Royal patronage, inter-denominational goodwill, distinguished members drawn from all walks of life, and the genius of the founder Padre Tubby Clayton, created and maintained a memorial to the fallen of the Somme and Passchendaele, which differed altogether from the war memorials on the Continent. Instead of the German seriousness and pathos, with drums and fanfares, or the French Glory, these doctors, bankers, industrialists, trade unionists, lords, and Members of Parliament, pooled their resources with a frivolous lightness of touch. Though hitched to the Cross of Calvary the keynote was one of godly fun.

The influence of the universities in Toc H and elsewhere was strong. Oxford and Cambridge still yielded a crop of young men who brought their laughter to the slums at a time when social work had not yet been defined. They could have walked out of pictures by Perugino or Botticelli. They seemed to transfigure the dreary dirt of the cities with their beauty and elegance. They were magnetic, and the children and adolescents clustered around them in clubs and settlements. They took their charges to summer camps or accompanied whole families to the hop-fields or fruit gardens of England. In the crude smelly huts they offered medical first aid, and at the camp fire they performed religious services or sing-songs, which ended with 'Abide with Me'. Perhaps they were to represent the last vestige of English chivalry or romance.

My reaction to these students and their elders mixed admiration with indignation. I loved them for their generosity and their indestructible optimism. I smiled at their boastfulness, and I profited from their good vocabulary. Like Tubby Clayton himself, they were still links in the chain of good English spoken with effortless superiority. On the other hand, they seemed to be ignorant. Though this was the era of new poetry in England and a profusion of great works appeared in print, these young Christians disdained an interest in literature, drama, art, or music. Perhaps they even identified the Christian call with a simplicity of mind which, if it heard of Eliot, Proust, Kafka, Hemingway, Epstein, Schoenberg, must shut eyes and ears lest they be tainted. But these men were not anti-modern in matters of engineering, for they were practical and could apply themselves to repairs of cars and other mechanical needs. Their competence and their romantic idealism stood in no need of intellectual fodder. The wider field of the British Empire still beckoned to the young who wanted to build and plant abroad. They had a tradition in their blood-stream and few scruples to deter them. For them the Christian religion was also the divine comedy, though few, if any of them, would have read Dante. At night, in the fields of Kent, under a silent starry sky, in that merry fellowship, one could be forgiven for thinking that God was in his heaven and all well in the world.

45

6

APPEASEMENT

A Divine Comedy of our time has not yet been written. The attempt to interpret our social history in spiritual terms founders on our moral relativism. Dante paired the guilty with their sins in respective pouches of punishment, climbed in purgatory with the penitent, before he disclosed the celestial spheres of eternal bliss. When we look at the period before the Second World War we witness the opening of the abyss towards which the proud and cruel dragged civilization, aided by the traitors and liars, and followed by the stupid and cowardly. I witnessed the descent into hell in London, still the centre of a benevolent insouciance. As the Nazi jackboot marched into the Rhineland, Austria, and the Sudetenland, as Abyssinia fell to Mussolini's armies, and the Spanish Civil War brought Fascist victories, this hell enlarged its mouth. We students, emerging from St James's Park into the Mall on the way to King's College in the Strand, passed the German embassy. The Nazis raised their flag and the 'Horst Wessel Lied' boomed across the Mall with arrogant confidence. How could the Divine Comedy find a place not only for all the villains (Hitler and Stalin would lie well in the ice), but all the good souls who went on praying for peace and, in the last resort, cared more deeply for the test-matches against Australia and were incensed by body-bowling?

I could never descend into the Inferno to place the culprits there, for apart from our inability to assess the guilt of individuals, it is our fate that we never meet our murderers and traitors. We only read about them, and we suffer from those who execute their orders. Nevertheless the editor of *The Times* (Dawson) represents that particular brand of English devilry, who under the cloak of impartiality furthered the cause of the appeasement of Hitler. He did this largely by suppressing unpleasant news. He also gave a slant to public opinion by publishing mainly only those letters to the editor which agreed with his policy. No letter of mine, or similar statements, ever appeared in print. Thus there grew up a solid body of respectable and very Christian persuasion which identified peace with appeasement. Nazi Antisemitism gave a flavour of specific poison to this 'Catholic' position, which had a broad range of support from such different writers as Eliot, Pound, Belloc, Chesterton. Shaw and the secularists formed an unholy alliance in this hell of self-deception, and soon the Communists joined the merry-go-round. Mosley and his Fascists never gained popularity, because they openly supported the barbarism, which the others wished to disguise by their devotion to tradition, humanism, pacifism, and socialism. The enemies of appeasement stood naked, without a spiritual halo.

But self-deception did not stop there, for false hopes obsess also the despairing. Though approaching the abyss they cannot realize the degree of perdition. The irony of the thirties during the Spanish Civil War may be compared to that of Job struggling against God, little knowing that he was the object of a wager between God and Satan. Just as Job pleads for himself in the hope of being heard, so the Left looked to Stalin as the upholder of freedom. It was an odd choice, far more outrageous than turning the poacher into the gamekeeper. One particular advocate of this false hope was the Communist Dean of Canterbury, Hewlett Johnson, a beautiful man and clever. On Whit Sunday I sat at his feet, spellbound, listening to this radical message of good cheer. Never has hell looked more like heaven than on that glorious Sunday with the light streaming through the thirteenth-century glass. It took many lives, betrayed at the front outside Madrid, and later the testimony of Orwell, to end the fable of the United Front and to replace it by the true legend of Comrade Napoleon.

My hopes collapsed as the Republican cause went towards defeat. The Spanish hierarchy with papal support and Nazi aeroplanes and Fascist soldiers shared in Franco's triumph. Guernica was bombed, but whilst this horror inspired Picasso to paint the huge picture, an indictment of the common enemy, Catholic opinion gloried in the developing anti-Communist crusade. Demagogues, such as Fr Coughlin who broadcast regular tirades for his Radio League of the Little Flower, the Irish Republican Army, many German friendship groups, intimidated the Christian conscience. The net, I knew, was closing, and I felt its spiritual power throttling and paralysing the men of truth.

Strangely enough, not all were subjected to, or felt, the tentacles of evil. Those around Churchill, though a minority, remained unshaken. More remarkable still, the German exiles in America, though surrounded by a vigorous native faction of pro-Nazis, pinned their hope on Roosevelt. The American President was for them the great righteous statesman, who combines wisdom with power, is dedicated to universal freedom and has the will to achieve it. Roosevelt became in his own day almost beatified among the intellectuals. Thomas Mann, for example, and Einstein looked to him, as a Dante would look to Henry VII of Luxembourg. The real Roosevelt, now known to history, was a far shrewder and less idealistic politician than his idolaters imagined. Indeed, without Japanese provocation he and his country would have stayed out of the war. But he fulfilled for his generation the role of a focus, the vision of a redeemer, the oracle that cannot fail. When the world could have collapsed entirely, not only to the force of arms but also to the supremacy of the lie, Roosevelt and the great republic in the west sustained the overarching belief that truth and power cannot for ever remain divided.

Without this conviction evidenced by an inner faith the human race enters hell on this earth, without even the prospect of purgatory. In the thirties it seemed to many that history is the record of despair. The victims of Stalin's purges, old comrades of the revolution, attained to the lowest depths, for they were not only tortured and murdered, but degraded, dishonoured, and totally annihilated as persons. They recanted and confessed. They stooped to every conceivable self-accusation and gave false testimony as dictated. While the Spanish Civil War raged there were held trials in Moscow which fulfilled the wildest dreams of Macbeth and Richard III and Iago. The unbelievable, the impossible, the non-existent were set up as real and true. The total reversal of all values took place, and mankind assented. Since my brother had emigrated to the USSR and his letters, already infrequent and empty before, ceased altogether I knew that he had been 'liquidated'. This word 'liquidation' described the process. Not only bones, blood, sinews, and flesh were boiled down to nothing, but the spirit of man was reduced to nothing.

I had good reason to pursue the study of theology. No business or success could interest me, if there was no world in which to live. I must find out about God, though I had to give up banking, quarrel with my mother, and still qualify by passing tiresome exams. The question of all questions pressed upon me through the world: Does God exist?

7

THE BASTION OF TRUTH

King's College in the Strand had been founded in 1829 with the active support of the Duke of Wellington. It represented the Christian establishment's answer to the free-thinking University College in Gower Street. In this way Anglicans countered the humanistic utilitarianism of Jeremy Bentham. But the strife, as so often in England, was less ideological than might be supposed, and the rivalry comic rather than deadly. The real issues of theological controversy were debated within King's College and led to one major scandal. In 1853 the Professor of Theology, F.D. Maurice, was deprived of his chair. The doctrine of eternal punishment stood between him and Principal R.W. Jelf. Maurice, though traditional through and through, picked holes in the dogma which Jelf and his friends were unwilling to soften. The sacked professor came well out of the struggle. Not only did he become Professor of Moral Philosophy at Cambridge and a champion of the working men and their education, but until this day he remains the exponent of an enlightened, if somewhat ponderous, theology. The present chair of moral theology at King's College is named after him.

No battles raged when I timidly approached the Dean's office to register as an ill-qualified student. Even the theological department, Anglican and paid for out of Church funds, and the secular faculties, funded by the state, worked together in harmony. The original charter had been emended so as to enable all the faculties to work and prosper within the University of London. A.C. Headlam, former Principal of the College, and a notable theologian to boot, had achieved this settlement, before he became Bishop of Gloucester (1923-45).

Headlam, though no longer physically present in London, came to worry me a great deal. Here was a highly gifted prelate, of outstanding integrity, an apostle of Christian unity committed to international understanding, who sided publicly with the near-Fascist advocacy of friendship with Nazi Germany. He presented me with the hard problem of the discernment of righteousness. Many weak and muddled people sense the wrong and usually avoid it, but strong minds side with a party which offends our simple moral instincts. How is this possible? Headlam, for example, stood for a very English Christianity and, because of his love for tradition and authority, fell into the trap of shibboleths, such as 'church', 'home', 'country'.

Doubtless the devotion to law and order and a loathing of anarchy make traditionalists victims to the *poseurs* in the political game. They are easily caught. Headlam was not alone in supping with the devil, accepting a very small spoon of poison before the whole infected meal is served up. Pétain and the Vichy regime were soon to follow and never seem to have become conscious of the spider's web into which they walked. Did they follow a blind instinct? Or did their collaboration extend to an acceptance of Nazi ideology? The case of Pius XII is famous. He moved on a much grander level and bowed to his blackmailers in an even more complex network of interests. Dante never invented pouches for men of such spiritual format who defend laudable interests with good intentions and are thereby sucked into a vortex of moral confusion.

Ascetic appearance and good breeding are, alas, no guarantee of good judgement. Even ascetic practice does not ensure a good heart. The goodness which I found at King's College was rooted in human generosity and understanding. Walter Matthews and Charles Gore, though now absent (one as Dean of St Paul's, the other in the next world), had left a stamp of genius on the department. Both had wrestled with the human side of Christianity without abandoning the transcendent givenness of the faith. Both had not only admitted the revolutionary facts of the twentieth century but welcomed them into the doctrinal re-shaping of belief. They were open spirits and minds, who avidly devoured the new science, literature, and psychology. Gore was the more demonic character, a monk who had founded the Community of the Resurrection and had served the Church as a bishop. He had the rare insight of equating the spiritual demand of God with a free response. Yet he also resisted the unbridled individualism of the age and sympathized with a form of socialism which respected the freedom of the individual. Hence he could not but be a utopian thinker, but his utopian framework stood firmly on experience and knowledge. He taught as a semi-retired bishop at King's (1919-30) at the invitation of Matthews, who without money or other advantages, had after the war re-established the department, and thus theology, in the University. Matthews's spirit still lingered in the old fashioned, high-ceilinged rooms.

The spirituality of those years before the war was curiously uncomplicated. It stemmed from a feeling of obligation. Worship pertained to God and also gave pleasure. Among our seniors a little pomposity alienated me. The Warden's tea-parties were dreaded and later laughed at for their formality. But the individual touch varied enormously. Eric Abbott, chaplain of the college and later Dean of Westminster, re-lieved the stiffness in the gloomy corridors with an elegant and witty solicitude for each student. He preferred lame dogs to prize-winners, and in my alienated state I gratefully accepted his care, until I noted its limitations. Underneath the attention I discovered an avoidance of real intimacy. At-traction, friendship, and passion were not allowed to out-grow the given frontiers. You could not weep on anyone's bosom, for we were reserved, and this reserve sprang from the Stoic tradition of English public schools. It tolerated much, but it did not feed the ecstasy or longing of the soul. Nor of the body: the power of sex must be channelled into mar-riage at some future date, or repressed in celibacy. Thus the beefy undergraduate who played rugger with verve could pray in chapel, help with clubs, a laughing and drinking cava-lier, deaf to the apocalyptic massing of forces in the out-side world.

The academic curriculum was vast: God himself alone could know the answers to the questions in biblical papers, Church history, doctrine, philosophy, and liturgy. The emphasis was always on facts, and the method of learning consisted of listening to lectures, taking notes, and reading. Examinations tested the memory. As the papers were absurdly long for three hours there was little opportunity to discuss problems. No one had yet discovered seminars, and tutor-ials, in imitation of the old universities, proved inadequate.

No one questioned the system; we accepted the menu as served. But there was a safety valve for frayed nerves. The cinema provided the needed antidote for very little money. I loved the great American epics. Greta Garbo inflamed every heart. I nearly died of laughter as I watched the Marx Brothers in *A Night at the Opera*. Even pictures of the marching Nazis in the News triggered off laughter. Being uncritical we accepted entertainment as escapism, and I discovered with glee that the Hebrew writers prayed for escape from the snare, the pit, and the hunter. I therefore accepted the charge that religion was escapism with the retort that all good things, including laughter, were a means of escape, to be cultivated and treasured.

But theology tends to ignore comedy. Our texts were serious and our teachers concentrated on grammar, syntax, and linguistic problems at the expense of exegesis. The classical background still dominated our unstable world, but the choice of books left much to be desired. The great tragedies played no part in our education, and Dionysius and the demonic-ecstatic remained out of view. However, Plato and Virgil furthered our moral and aesthetic education, and Cicero's classical *Somnium Scipionis* made me conscious of a graded and adorable universe in which all things work out for the best. Pagan antiquity buttressed an optimistic evaluation of the cosmos, and this was a relief as events unfolded before one. I knew this Dream by heart and was shattered when I learnt that Cicero, for all his pains, was murdered by Mark Antony's butchers. Our Roman history was sketchy and conveyed in jocular fashion, and the misdeeds of Sulla and Nero were written off as comic turns. But when it came to the end of Cicero all my fears returned. How could the good man, the philosopher, defend himself against the mob and the gangsters in power? Was the Dream the answer for us all?

No, paganism and pagan writers gave no protection against the enemy. I turned to the biblical texts instead. Their authority was still regarded as final. The bishops never tired of telling the Church and the country that renewal would come through the knowledge of, and devotion to, the Bible. The Bible had made England what she was, however philistine in art and music. I had come a long way from my days at school: instead of the denigration of that 'Jewish book' under the sign of the swastika the scriptures not only promised salvation in the future but even here and now.

Yet as we got into the texts — Psalms in Hebrew, Gospels in Greek — and faced problems, such as different readings, I lost my simple assurance. Scholarship opposed a simple literalism, though in some colleges they still dated Adam some four millennia before Christ, claimed that the Flood left only Noah and his remnant in the ark, regarded the Exodus from Egypt as an intervention by God's strong hand, and tolerated no doubt about the collapse of Jericho's walls at the blast of the trumpet, nor of the sun's standing still over the valley of Ajalon. But this was precisely the question, especially as Hitler pounced on one of his victims after another: where was the miraculous power?

A different air pervaded King's College. S.H. Hooke, a formidable Semitic scholar, who had been brought up as a Plymouth Brother, had now reacted against fundamentalist sectarianism. He stood for the discipline of objective historical criticism and the comparative study of religion. Ever since Frazer's *The Golden Bough* (1911--1932) the English had digested lessons of worldwide religious phenomena with eager interest. In the days of Empire scholars like Robertson Smith had travelled in Arabia and collected evidence from the desert. Hooke now developed the techniques of his predecessors and united with them the theories of the German pioneers, such as Gunkel. Form-criticism was added to the literary criticism of the Bible and opened a new perspective to interpretation. Oesterley brought the knowledge of folklore and primitive religions into the field. In short, the history and religion of Israel were no longer divorced from the Middle East and its archaeology. The digs just begun at ancient Ugarit contributed a new, even sensational, element. Yet Hooke delivered all these finds in a sad and monotonous voice. Unhappy at the time and in marital distress he undermined the Bible as a disclosure of the divine, for he had lost his faith.

These negative results did not disturb the students unduly. That Moses adopted a tribal god called Yah; that the prophets were ecstatics, magicians, politicians; that sacrifice was barbaric throughout; that many heroes, like Samson, had once been gods; that the covenant was one among many; that the priests were cultic officials who served a king, who was god; that this king performed a seasonal myth-ritual in which he died and rose again after a fight in the underworld — all these sceptical evaluations of the text were noted for the examinations and then laid aside as irrelevant to our condition.

However, the problem could not be evaded altogether, for what was true of the Old Testament must somehow apply also to the New. Our conservative teacher, however, chose not to get embroiled. We learnt about the Jewish-Hellenistic-Roman world as a matter of history, and then fitted in Jesus and Paul as best we could. The names and books of dangerous form-critics, such as Dibelius, Bultmann, and Schmidt, were never mentioned. Even Dodd was too much associated with godless Cambridge. Unencumbered by exegetical problems we became acquainted with highly technical methods of textual criticism. I felt disenchanted. One day, with enthusiasm, I approached the professor to ask him about the passage in John 'Before Abraham was I am', which I recognized to contain the mystery of pre-existence. He was irritated and left me bewildered. The New Testament, too, was encapsulated in and through technical expertise. Unknown to us, we were victims of historicism at a time when history was on the march.

Perhaps it was as well that the English refused to get sucked into the sterile debate about the Bible. A sovereign and free way of dealing with the Gospels came refreshingly from William Temple. He embodied in his big frame the genius of English Christianity. His visits to the College attracted vast crowds. He was the hero of our generation, without being a hero; the saint of our epoch, without the marks of clerical sanctity; the outstanding scholar and theologian, who disdained pedantic littleness; the leader, who shunned an appeal to the mob; the socialist, who could only be thought of as a member of the ruling class. Temple was Olympian. Like his archbishop father he could be conservative and modern. He was almost boyish in his enthusiasm, fatherly in his warmth, brotherly in his identification with the people. He was not a good judge of people, for he assumed in others the natural goodness and absence of guile which ordered his life. He laboured like a giant. After a day's work he would take up his writing and continue a sentence, broken off in the middle, without having to re-read the words preceding the gap. Temple was not only the spokesman of Anglicanism at its best, but of England before the war. Pacifist at heart, and utterly given over to ecumenical co-operation, he nevertheless sensed, and then opposed, the barbarism across the Channel. But his stand was by no means as clearsighted as Churchill's, and these two geniuses, so typical of English life, never had much in common.

Temple's writings have become part of the great tradition, even if they have not weathered well after his death. Temple is an idealist philosopher. From *Mens Creatrix* to *Readings in St John's Gospel* he never wavers in his quiet and majestic assumption that there is an eternal Transcendence, that all being is derived from this Being who is God, and that all men are destined to attain to the knowledge of the truth because it is irresistible. The revelation of God in Christ is the Word of truth dwelling in our midst, and the Spirit declares the truth of Christ in the Church. Temple's whole edifice stands coherently, rationally, and delightfully on traditional evidence and personal witness and experience. History does not present the insoluble problem to Temple who views it, as does the evangelist, from an eternal point of view. Temple could be called a Hellenistic Christian, but he eschews gnostic tendencies and mystical extravagances. He is at heart as much a realist as he is an idealist, and in this respect his writings perpetuate his unforgettable presence. If I learnt anything through him it was the lesson of Jesus, neither idea nor even ideal, but Logos made flesh, as John insists. Temple infleshed the Lord for a large and grateful world.

Temple's *Readings in St John's Gospel* may be regarded as his testament and also as the epitome of the best spiritual treasures of an age. 'It has no distinctive and consistent character' says the author by way of introduction. Just because Temple is not concerned with the minutiae of exposition, and yet always aware of scholarly points at issue, he can allow himself the freedom of 'what the Holy Spirit says to me through the Gospel'. The result is orderly and poetic, systematic and free, traditional and unpredictable. Temple, the philosopher, does not shun the Palestinian character of his great love. 'In the temporal event we behold the eternal reality' — what more is there to say?

'Christianity is the most materialistic of all great religions' is the famous reply of Temple's, a reply which deeply affected the generation which listened to him. Thereby he not only saves the churches' sacramentalism from magic, and the accusation of cheap credulity, but also imparts to the sick world the means of healing. Typically, Temple places the Johannine Christ at the centre of all salvation. This Christ is neither 'liberal' nor 'apocalyptic', and is only 'Messiah' in the sense of being the author and perfecter of the Kingdom of God. Power is in complete subordination to Love. Hence suffering and sacrifice.

I have telescoped Temple's magisterial English to show the nature of the mature Christian who faced the events of 1939. He eschewed all propaganda and sentimentality. He had no truck with sectarian models. He did not parade learning. He put the eternal Christ in our midst as the only and lasting sanction for truth and service. It is amazing how Temple narrows the focus lest the Gospel be swallowed up in secular interpretation. Instead, the world is interpreted by the Gospel, and since we are in the world and of the world, he teaches us not only to serve, but to be served.

One could hardly arrive at the date of the composition of this commentary from the internal evidence. The world is an empty stage and we do not even hear the rumbling of guns or the whine of diving planes. 'The world is groping after its true leader; he offers himself; and the world, after yielding for a moment to the impact of his divinity, arrests him and crucifies him.' Not a word about the Führer or the Duce, not even an allusion to their claims. The Archbishop's ordeal only shines through a few lines, such as 'The divine kingdom can never fight for its "vital interests", because by fighting it betrays them.' There is the rub, and Temple adds 'The State may rightly fight in national self-defence or for the maintenance of the law of the nations'. But for this concession England could hardly have declared war on Hitler.

Though highly sensitive to the complexities of the relationship between men and states, of power and love, Temple
avoids the usual theological dialectic. He must be simple, and
an astonishing simplicity strikes the reader after some forty
years. On the famous 'What is truth?' Temple quotes Bacon's
equally famous 'Jesting Pilate would not stay for an answer'.
Then he concludes: 'But it is better to stay and wait for the
answer'. Here is the theologian, preacher, moralist, and man
in a nutshell. He conveyed a simplicity of belief which could
still operate in men's hearts.

Thus Temple can, for his generation, interpret death and
crucifixion with unequalled seriousness and brevity. It seems
almost as if the writer does not wish to get between God's
sufferings and his readers. His modesty forbids him to beat
the breast and lament. He feels the pain, but he does not
allow the pain to be sensational or morbid. The pain is not
evaded, and the death is not a charade. Nor is it simply the
debt paid to nature or to the devil. Rather, it pertains to the
darkness, and this darkness passes into the dawn and the
dawn heralds the light. Temple replies to the dark powers,
without naming them or exploring the depths of their
demonic degradation and horror.

Temple was not demonic and did not know experientially
the dark side of human nature. Kenneth Kirk, by contrast,
was not only academic through and through but also a tough,
even dictatorial, prelate. Later when he was my diocesan I
suffered from, and also admired, his Yorkshire hardness. He
humiliated church officers by deliberately making them
wait upon him in a cold room, and when they were nearly
frozen he dismissed them curtly. He himself suffered from
acute melancholia. A widower, he had been left to care for
his many children. He would rest in a darkened vicarage,
sometimes for several days. He loved good food and drink
and did not despise hard-earned wealth. He was not only
a big man in every sense of the word, but he knew himself
to be big. He loved village congregations and preached simple
sermons in which he quoted from Bunyan's *Pilgrim's Progress*.
Yet he was the staunchest Catholic, a visitor to Nashdom
Abbey and a friend of the monks. Kirk was a split personality, highly complex, and a rarity among English bishops,

among whom he seemed isolated.

His lectures on moral problems were caustic and brilliant. His elegant rhetoric enhanced the impact of his invective. He was not at all disposed to back up English humanism and to submit to a united front with all men of good will. Men, he affirmed, were not crocodiles who acted upon the instinct of swallowing the nearest morsel that offered, but they were free. The nature of this freedom he knew to be highly problematical. In *The Vision of God* of 1928, one of the few theological works of the century in English which will survive, he gave an immense survey of the tradition behind the promise. They shall see God. The vision of God, from Moses to Pascal and beyond, invites the reader to visit the peaks of our civilization and thus to delineate a Christian humanism. Kirk taught me that there is in theology, as in philosophy, a dialectic without which we cannot understand anything, not even ourselves. Our best masters are often those with whom we cannot agree and whose views we must regard as mischievous or malevolent. Thus the vision of God eludes direct description. Claims and actions contradict each other. The ascetics hurl insults at the worldlings, but the extremists discredit themselves by their fanaticism. The war between the factions of Christians, of the major orders, of the national groups, of outstanding saints, and then of East and West, Protestant and Catholic, Christian and secular — this war, as one learnt from Kirk, pertains to our peace. No glory without the cross, not even the cross of misunderstanding and tragic breakdown. Kirk, unlike Temple, did not rise above the struggle, but brought the struggle into the arena of Christian spirituality.

From all quarters there flowed streams of, and towards, a Christian humanism, and we young students gave it a great welcome. It was the English antidote to the totalitarian brutalism. It flourished at High Mass, with incense and baroque music. It induced fasts, especially before Communion, and pilgrimages, as to Walsingham, to venerate the Virgin and all the saints. The world belonged to God, and we as stewards gave physical expression to the spiritual essence, even to the point of dressing-up and childish rituals.

St Thomas Aquinas of the thirteenth century became the

unquestioned authority for this sacramental teaching. It was up-dated and called neo-Thomism. In fact, people did not read too much of the *Summa Theologiae* (then called Theo-logica) nor did they delight greatly in the somewhat monoton-ous argument *pro* and *contra*. This rational step-by-step argu-ment commended itself more directly to the great French-men of the epoch. A galaxy of theologians — Maritain, Gil-son, Sertillanges and others — developed this Christian humanism in a manner unsurpassed to this day. When they lectured in the uncomfortable Large Theatre of our College we were taken into the heart of theology itself. What is ana-logy? What is language? What is Being? They not only asked, but also answered, these hair-raising questions.

Neo-Thomism did not evade the problems of our exist-ence. It blended eternal objectivity and subjective needs in such a convincing fashion that one could only marvel that the world was not a better place. Maritain, in particular, with a Jewish-Christian wife, showed a fine sensitivity for our poli-tical dangers. In his *Degrees of Knowledge* he interpreted the degrees of Being and Becoming as related to our perception and experience of reality. Such a system helped to make one feel less wounded by the triumphant irrationalism which blared out of totalitarian loudspeakers. We were drawn to this civilized form of Catholicism, in which the great French cathedrals seemed to open their portals again for all the persecuted. The tradition, so it seemed, was on our side. But it was not to be: the Spanish War mocked and ended the progress of this enlightened and humane philosophy of religion. The champions of St Thomas had to find a refuge in the universities of the United States. Europe was no longer a place for the intellectual virtues of *consonantia, integritas,* and *claritas.* But even in Europe one could still recall that 'the temporal is subordinate to the spiritual plane', that 'action (even ours) is an epiphany of being', and that 'the most terrible anguish for a Christian is precisely this of knowing that there can be justice in the use of hor-rible means'. Even as Madrid fell all was not lost.

8

THE SPIRIT OF MUNICH

As the year 1938 approached and we took our finals in June we forgot about external and eternal claims. It is amazing how human beings can restrict their horizon to the tiniest speck with an urgency and concentration which stand in inverse proportion to their importance, at least in the eyes of the rest of the world. However, examinations come and go, but the trial of man remains. These tests are a reminder of the fact that we stand at the bar of history, and that our ordeal is not unconnected with a last assizes when every man must give an account of himself, whether good or bad. The King's College prayer daily reminds its members of their appearing at length before the judgement seat to settle these accounts. In 1938 no one questioned as yet the substance of this ethical vindication, be it in rewards or punishments.

The acceleration of events — the constant victories of the tyrants and their bold brutalities — did nothing to lessen the expectation of such a judgement. The mouth of hell opened with ever-increasing appetite. The descent was now swift, and suddenly the universal optimism waned noticeably. I spent the late summer at Lincoln for a term of final training. Fears of war could no longer be suppressed. The college was divided between pacifists and reluctant fighters. The latter knew that they would be exempt from military duties once they were ordained. Nevertheless, the ideological battle was joined with some heat.

The anti-war party had the advantage that they sounded to themselves more 'Christian'. But apart from this emotional advantage the neo-Thomist school brought reason to bear upon the issue. My friend Eric Mascall, who was to become a theologian of note, sprang an impressive defence for the 'lesser evil', which, if I remember rightly, was not war, but peace. If we submitted to Nazi claims we were doing the right thing, since a war would no longer be 'rational'. It would cause greater havoc than any defence we could muster. In other words, military inferiority became now a reasoned argument for submission. It had first been caused by appeasing tendencies and was now used to give a plausible backing-up for metaphysical notions of good and evil. It seemed to me then, as it does now, the most immoral of all arguments, inasmuch as it creates a moral climate by doing nothing, and then exploiting the disastrous state of general indolence for moral pleading. In this way the word 'peace' becomes the kind of mockery which Jeremiah had already detected, in a different context, when his enemies used the slippery word to intrigue in spurious alliances.

At Lincoln there remained a stalemate, and the reconciliation between the factions was found in worship, work, and tennis. The cinema down the hill also helped to allay ruffled feelings. But I remained highly disturbed and was not helped by an encounter with the highly respected Charles Williams, the author of books on Christian apologetic. I remember facing him alone in Eric Abbott's drawing room and questioning him closely. 'What now?' I demanded in a forthright manner. Chamberlain had begun his flying visits to Germany to 'solve' the Sudetenland crisis. Charles Williams had written, and was still writing, on hell and heaven. He knew the threat of the demonic. But his answers were evasive, and I was bitterly disappointed. No clarion-call, no recognition, no intuition! If only he and his friends would come clean, I thought, and simply state their case for self-preservation! Why invoke God and adopt theological postures when all you really want is to look after your own skin?

My state was not helped by my spiritual adviser. He was well known in Anglo-Catholic circles and regarded as very sound. I made my confession, which must have been a mixture of contrition and fury. He replied coolly. My mistake, he fluted, was to take these political events and ideological reactions so seriously. They were crowding out the real object of life, the knowledge and love of God. He really rebuked me, without knowing it, for being what I was. He exposed to me a spirituality which is typical of many 'little books', whose pedigree goes back to none less than Thomas à Kempis and even St François de Sales. Bouquets of flowers and a contempt of the world were to feed the Jesus-centred soul.

Such postures ill accorded with the climax or anticlimax in foreign affairs. Chamberlain flew to Munich and with Hitler, Daladier, and Mussolini signed the infamous piece of paper. It is now no longer fashionable to identify the leaders and their henchmen who tainted their names by the smiling betrayal of Czechoslovakia. A witchhunt after these many years serves no purpose, but the shame of a false theology remains. Here was an exquisite example of false prophecy. Every ingredient of pious treachery, in the name of God, could be heard, seen, and felt. The darkness lay over the whole land, and only a very few lights remained. The piece of paper which promised 'Peace in our Time' was shown, admired, and believed in. Protests were not reported, but pictures of hysterical and jubilant crowds filled the pages. Never was so much relief felt for so little easing of pain. Delusion fed upon delusion. God, so it was said, had come to our aid. On the Sunday following the news the Dean of Lincoln preached at a solemn thanksgiving service. He held the congregation spellbound by ascribing the turn of events to God's wonderful providence. I ran out of my stall and feeling sick to the point of convulsion I gazed at the great west façade of the cathedral. The façade, in all its magnificence, is a sham, for it is not integral to the nave behind it. I saw in it the empty gesture of false prophecy.

The year which followed — in which I was ordained and recovered from the collapse — is perhaps the most interesting of our spiritual history. It is also the most hidden. The political and military development somehow went against the expectation of Chamberlain and Halifax. The country slowly woke up from its dreams and accepted rearmament. Spitfires and Hurricanes began to come off the production line. The rehearsal for evacuation in 1938 had prepared the civilian population for another crisis. The whole feeling changed. But the Church still dragged its feet. On the parochial level I endured the whole of the muddle. At the Armistice Service, attended by the British Legion, I was produced as an exhibit for reconciliation with the Germans. The real cause why I was in the English pulpit would have been suppressed if I had not invoked St Paul's 'Are they Hebrews? So am I'. Curiously enough, this outburst was well received, and even the clergy did not protest. Their pacific attitude was based as much upon ignorance as on bad theology, and once they heard my cause they were quite ready to be swayed. But the battle was prolongued, for the Vicar was bitten with the bug of the Oxford Group Movement, and this strange and somewhat formidable organization wanted to include Hitler and Himmler in its Moral Rearmament. The Vicar, therefore, offered from the heart prayers for the conversion of the German leadership. Such a prayer fed the illusion that such men had still to make a choice. It was also dangerous ammunition because it contained a parallel clause in which we prayed for the conversion of our own men, who favoured war instead of peace. In this manner Churchill was put on the same moral level as Hitler.

But theologically the most insidious influence, because new to me, came from the Spanish mystics. My Vicar was rather un-typical for an English clergyman. He had been a professional soldier and as a former officer he could not but be attracted by St Ignatius and the hard rule of life. A soldier of Christ must not only obey but harden himself by austerities. One of these was the practice of minimal sleep. Fortified with black tea we would sit up in the tiny kitchen of the council house on a huge L.C.C. estate, and he would with hypnotic eyes and affection infiltrate the teachings of self-laceration. St John of the Cross, rather than St Theresa of Avila, figured here as the hero of a total immolation of self. Hitler and Churchill, war or peace, freedom or tyranny, and all other options were now pushed aside as meaningless and even as diabolical seductions. Our duty was towards God. He could be found, and only found, in and through the Christ who was crucified and died. The death that really mattered was the death of our mind, for we were drawn by our sinful imagination towards patterns which were idolatrous. I went to bed with my head reeling, and after only two hours' sleep we gathered in the mysterious light before the altar. There was the Light of the World.

The National Gallery helped me to put flesh on this tempting Spanish mysticism. There is Velasquez's *Immaculate*

Conception in which the whole warring globe is put under the feet of the Virgin. The Catholic newspapers tried to equate this picture with the result of Franco's victories. They suppressed the Moorish share in the campaigns, not to mention the Nazi and Fascist legions. Thus was I torn between what I wanted to believe, and the knowledge of what I knew to be true. Goya's pictures seemed a little more to the point. His scenes of war, with their portrayal of the ruthless infliction of misery, rang true at this time of final defeat.

But English spirituality was in no better state to help me. King Edward's abdication had taken place, but this turned out to be a hollow victory for the Church. The mental paralysis after Munich tainted even the best endeavours of the pious, who exalted Chamberlain as their apostle of peace. The prophets of the age chose to excommunicate themselves. Auden and Isherwood, for example, left for America. The narrowness of English conventions was matched by the insipidity of secular thought. To me it seemed that cricket acted as a kind of common denominator of wilful blindness.

9

MORAL REARMAMENT

The European disease of the spirit was not confined to the old Continent, but we were insular enough to think that it must be. This European insularity fed, and then fed upon, the American isolationism which was by no means lessened through the Wall Street crash. Even the election of President Roosevelt hardly pierced the hostile isolationism of the Middle West. The 'American Firsters' had an understandable bias against European entanglements and the Monroe doctrine buttressed their stand with respectable ancestry. Charles Lindbergh, who had for the first time crossed the Atlantic in an aircraft alone in 1927, opposed American aid to the anti-Nazi democracies.

Nevertheless, as we approached the final precipice the Voice of America whispered into some ears the hope that a solution might be found, in which peace and justice would be triumphant. Roosevelt contributed his fair share to kindling such a hope. Ever since the days of his inauguration when he had coined the famous phrase 'The only thing we have to fear is fear itself' he had shown himself capable of action to implement the hope of the Fair Deal. The words in which his legislation was enshrined pointed the way forward to that 'active faith' which the President also sustained in his fireside chats. Labour was to be used with fairness, security was to be social. The reforms were not verbal but tangible and visible. This American way of doing things proved once again that faith and works can and must go together. The intellectual element is only secondary, even if, as in Roosevelt's case, it was headed by the Brains Trust. The members of this body were remarkable for their independence and provided the Administration with a charismatic continuity. Roosevelt's oracles and Hopkins's memoranda paved the way to the recovery. But they did not alter the climate of isolation.

However, the Christian leaders of the great institutions, such as the interdenominational Union Theological College in New York, provided the spiritual leadership which proved prophetic. They had to contend with conservative prejudice and pacifist obscurantism. Outstanding and of lasting eminence remains Reinhold Niebuhr (1892—1971), who became a professor at Union in 1928 and taught until 1960. His work became known in England before and during the war. He was a religious pragmatist who scorned the humbug of optimistic illusions and cheap evasions. He believed in freedom, reason, and love — the very qualities of life which were now ridiculed and about to be stamped out by the totalitarian states. Pride and sensuality had always been triumphant in history, but to yield to their arrogant and meaningless assertions was to abdicate all responsibility. As an American and as a Christian Niebuhr analysed man's moral situation to give him the courage to stand.

The case of Europe was, therefore, not to be dismissed as a foreign irrelevance. The dialectic of meta-historical love and the claims of justice addressed all mankind. Now moral man had to defend himself against immoral society. The book *Nature and Destiny of Man* appeared when the Japanese bombs on Pearl Harbour had already settled the issue, but Niebuhr's prophetic voice had not been heard in vain before. Reviewing the religious and secular dimensions of modern life in 1958, in *The Godly and the Ungodly*, Niebuhr analyses the historical contingency under Roosevelt and the strange victory, which was needed for moral reasons, over liberalism 'informed by pacifistic, moralistic, and isolationist illusions'. He demonstrates the interdependence of religious belief and moral obligation in this tragic conflict, in which we are meant to be creators as well as creatures.

Niebuhr spoke as a Christian in *Beyond Tragedy*. These 'sermonic essays' reached England after Munich and may well have helped to redress the balance after the great spiritual capitulation. Here he walked the tightrope as an accomplished artist, yielding to the temptation neither of pietistic otherworldliness nor of thundering bellicosity. He reinterpreted our role in history, 'as deceivers, yet true', and thus hitched our perilously lurching Christian responsibility to an inescapable moral obligation.

I am not sure that the actors in the Divine Comedy of 1939 were consciously aware of moral obligations stated in Niebuhr's terms. Halifax, no doubt, would have accepted them and come to a diametrically opposed policy. Others would have arrived at Niebuhr's political stance without subscribing to his principles. At that time I became uncomfortably aware of the gulf which separates men from principles, principles from action, and, above all, individuals from society. Niebuhr and Temple operated upon a pattern of general cohesion. But could you still adhere to any pattern when glaring fissures appeared? Could you not maintain, upon the grounds of experience, that there was simply an elemental force, and that principles were only covering up the random nature of what was happening? If this elemental force rose and fell, in the tidal manner explicated by Spengler, how could the individual stem this tide?

The stress of the times produced many prophets who pointed the way by offering a personal transcendantalism. If history threatens to swallow you up, they said in effect, you can transcend the bondage of historical existence. These chains are forged by our submission to generalization in all its horrible forms. We objectify the powers, we acknowledge the collective, we sign away our freedom. But refuse this act of spiritual apostasy and pledge your life to a dynamic, non-objective freedom, and you will already share in the indeterminate and cosmic reality. A godlike personalism, probing pure possibility and growing out of pure potentiality, turns the flanks of the impersonal slavery. However ghastly history, it can become tragic and therefore meaningful, for and through the aristocrats of the age, the persons who fulfil their individuality in freedom.

These aspirations and consolations came from many quarters when they were most needed. They were not as new as they sounded. Esoteric thinkers, such as Jacob Boehme, had described this cosmic essence of potential freedom and its attainment by men. Nicolas Berdyaev (1874—1948) added his sensitive interpretation of personalism to the chorus. Following a long tradition, and especially the work of Solovyev, he steered a bold way between unacceptable collectivism (socialism) and *entrepreneur* capitalism. For him personal freedom was not a selfish and eccentric possession but a state in which true community could be built. Undeterred by Russian opposition in the Soviet Union and among the émigrés in Paris he lived for this genuine *sobornost*. He lit a light in the darkness, unorthodox and fertilizing, especially for those who had to make no decisions whatever since, like him, they wielded no power.

In the twilight of 1939, which was soon felt to offer no more than a respite from war, personalism was as good a Christian salt as any to flavour the horrible stew around us. Personalism was concrete and could be taken at a deep philosophical level as well as in the daily round of hospitals, schools, and homes. It provided me with a private weapon, not only against the threat of war and totalitarian triumph, but also against the petty worries of parish-pump politics. Ecclesiastical machinery was not yet too overbearing, but it was good to pierce its armour with the freedom of the spirit, which sanctioned a different scheme of things. Here was a new disclosure of the destiny of man, which raised the 'I' to Him from whom it took its origin. According to Berdyaev God and man are apprehended, not in isolation, but through the personalistic metaphysics of the Holy Trinity. All this seemed difficult at first, but made sense even in one's pastoral duties and sufferings. I discovered, in short, that Russian feeling was not nearly as divorced from working-class life in England as was commonly assumed. On the vast estates of little houses, sunk in anonymity and poverty, the meaningless darkness yielded to the revelatory darkness of Dostoyevsky's fiction. I read *The Demons* and *The Brothers Karamazov* and began to see everything with new eyes.

In this vast Russian panorama, now applied to our world, there was little left of the Anglican spirit of tolerance and fun. I was engrossed in the vulgar debaucheries of Karamazov *père*, shared the suicidal despairs of Ivan, wept over the unjust sufferings of Dmitri, and identified with Alyosha's monastic devotion, his expulsion into the world of boys and prostitutes, and his quest for Christlike perfection. But this pattern of priesthood collided with the expectations among my colleagues. It was too exalted and interfered with Mothers Union and similar tea-drinking institutions. When Hitler marched into the Sudetenland I was seized by the prophetic afflatus and preached to the ladies about the imminent destruction. Looking beyond it I chose the text from Isaiah 58.12, 'They shall build the old wastes', taking for granted what must surely come. My audience did not like this at all and asked for my dismissal, which the Vicar refused to entertain. In him the old soldier was beginning to stir, and his visions agreed with mine, and contrasted with my fellow curate's uncompromising pacifism. But despite his backing I was shocked by the critique of my radical visions. They were further undermined when I received a visitor from the Home Office. This well-bred young man came to interview me in connection with my application for naturalization. He ridiculed my ideas and I wondered if I had passed his scrutiny. There would certainly be no war, he assured me in parting.

The summer of 1939 brought the relaxation before the inevitable climax. The air was hot. I cannot recall any overpowering spiritual event to counteract the depression. We were drifting. The Evian Conference on Refugees had showed convincingly that nothing can be done for people in danger. No one wanted to take the Jews, open a frontier for the persecuted. Palestine, the promised land, reduced its quotas under the aegis of the British Foreign Office.

I received an invitation from my mother to meet her in Chamonix. I had climbed Mont Blanc before, and as the train climbed through the meadows from St Gervais I lifted my eyes to the everlasting hills. The white domes and glaciers towered above in complete contrast to the world from which I had escaped on barely acceptable papers of identification and travel documents. Once again I sat gazing at this world, not yet polluted with endless high-rise properties, holiday villas, ski-lifts and mountain hotels. The air was pure. I read Karl Barth's commentary on the *Epistle to the Romans*. My father had sent me a copy, his last present to me. Sir Edwin Hoskyns had rendered the famous book into English in 1928, but it had not evoked a ripple of interest. But Barth had made a name for himself as perhaps the only theologian in Germany who had resisted the Nazis. He had been deprived of his post. He had returned to teach at Basel and we were to hear more of him.

This famous commentary which appeared at the end of the First World War, had shaken the liberal Protestant world. Harnack, as we have seen, had deplored Barth's radicalism. Even now in 1939, before the Second War, Barth rang the bells at midnight. Everything was theological and therefore polemical; nothing was simple or straightforward. Barth exposed the 'inner dialectic of the matter', which Paul sets forth in Romans, not only for his world but for us too. Here, under the blue sky in total stillness, I responded to a theology of crisis, which lifted our political crisis to God through Christ. Not that the result was cosy, for this dialectic of hope, and love, and, above all, faith made as much of the No as of the Yes. Barth wove a pattern of wondrous strands, as if Augustine, Aquinas, Kant, Dostoyevsky, and Kierkegaard helped the apostle to erect the infinite qualitative distinction between God and man, beyond which — and only beyond, not within — God declared himself for us in Christ. This modern God's dog (*Domini canis!*) not only barked up the right tree: he could also bite, as he had shown subsequently in the weakness of the Confessing Church.

One morning I returned from my reading, in which the discovery of the hitherto unknown Kierkegaard figured prominently. 'If we have died with Christ so we believe: we shall also live with him', was the text, and the commentary on this immense contradiction, duality, tension, polarity, antinomy, Either-Or, Both-And, Yes-No, awoke me finally out of the conventional slumber called religion. Barth broke with all human analogies and aspiration. Barth scorned the step-by-step arguments of the schoolmen, the *a fortiori* reasoning from the known to the unknown. Even the given aspects of personality, features of the inner life, or whatever psychological insights, did not promote our knowledge of God. On the contrary, God disclosed himself in the negation of our negation, in the acquittal of our guilt, in the resurrection of our dying. Our life is death, his death is our life. Death rules over aeons of developments, systems, religions, but life is the Other, unknown and revealed. The truth is not coherent, but paradoxical. Barth, who had hurled his defiant No! at Brunner and so-called natural theology, transcended the categories of

71

being, having, becoming, with the Pure Act of Revelation, Grace, and Resurrection.

Book in hand, I returned and saw the headings: Ribbentrop and Molotov Sign Pact. The pictures confirmed the hellish deed which must trigger off the explosion. Within a few hours a deathly silence descended upon the valley. No band played; the shutters came clattering down and were fastened. The tables in the cafés formed a circle and the chairs were placed above them. The last trains going north burst with passengers and piles of luggage.

During the night we stopped and started again. A grey mist over the fields obscured the landscape. We waited for the dawn in the corridors, black with the smuts of French coal. 'This is not far from Arras', said a military voice. A large war cemetery extended for miles and beyond. 'We held that stupid little hill', confirmed a cockney voice. Two ladies emerged from their first-class compartments as if nothing had happened, making their way to the ablutions. Two words alternated in my head: Death and Resurrection, Death and Resurrection. The train's rhythm spelt it out. We drew into the suburbs of Lille and came to a sharp stop opposite the barracks. They could be watched in the process of their mobilization. Small groups of *poilus* stood aimlessly around, a few horses were harnessed to some antique armoured vehicle. Those with eyes to see kept their forebodings in silence. Death yes, but Resurrection?

On 24 August of that year, unknown to me and most of my friends, Bonhoeffer wired the theme of his proposed Croall Lectures to John Baillie in Edinburgh: 'Death in the Christian Message'. They were never to be given, except in blood. He had returned from his friends and would-be benefactors in America, had visited and again left his relations in England, his decision firmly made to stand by his brothers in Christ. The invasion of Poland began on 1 September. Death or Resurrection? The question had ceased to be academic.

10

WAR AND PEACE

I felt spiritually well-equipped when the sirens whined the air-raid alarm on that blue bright Sunday morning of 3 September 1939. War was declared. Chamberlain had to make his sad, reluctant admission. No bombs were dropped on the occasion. The country which had hysterically hailed the peace of the year before accepted the state of war with dry equanimity. I felt relieved and read into this acceptance a spiritual dimension. I knew the dangers of 'God on our side' slogans, and it seemed that the Christian voice was hushed for that reason. There seemed to be almost a moratorium on enthusiasm. The usual clichés were, of course, bandied around, but the most memorable feature of the 'phoney war' until May 1940 was the spiritual vacuum. The reason was not far to seek: the prophets had been wrong and were not eager to confess the sin of their false words. The conservative clergy and laity alike had gathered around Chamberlain, wanting and shouting 'peace' in order to preserve their status, and the pacifists and idealists of the left had sentimentalized political realities. Both sides appropriately took a breather and kept silent. There was enough to occupy everyone with practical tasks, such as black-out, petrol and food rationing, evacuation of women and children. The reaction to war heightens the mental indolence of most people.

Soon I also had my full share of this spiritual paralysis. Now suddenly words and thoughts availed much less than arrangements for shelter. Once the initial excitement was over, and Poland easily overrun by Germany and Russia, the exhaustion of peace in wartime could be felt especially at religious services. I had never suffered from 'depression' until that dark, cold winter touched one's innermost being with non-being. Perhaps we were all the 'hollow men' of T.S. Eliot's poem.

My colleagues hit back at frustration. The Vicar, forgetting

all about St John of the Cross and setting aside Moral Rearmament, volunteered for active service. To his immense
chagrin the War Department told him to go home. But my
pacifist friend and fellow-curate was luckier and soon appeared
in Air Force blue to bid good-bye. For the first time, English
priests felt useless and questioned the validity not of their
orders but of the priestly *raison d'être*. They did not realize
at the time that a new abyss was beginning to open. What
'word' could match the present conflict, and who was to listen to it? What 'sacrament' could raise this flock of sheep
from going round in circles?

Other ideologies fared worse and showed themselves in
their true colours. The Fascists vanished from the scene and
their voices from the underground repeated Nazi anti-Semitic
slogans to little effect. They never gained the upper hand as
in north-west Europe. Possibly the hatred of traitors and the
contempt for treachery in England had something to do with
this remarkable fading away of a fifth column on the right.
On the left things were very different, for the Communists
and their allies openly proclaimed that this war deserved no
backing at all. The Third International trumpeted its slogans
against all monopolist-capitalist powers. It was to be inferred
that the western allies were the aggressors and that the Reich
was put on the defensive. Thus Stalin and Molotov carried out
their part of the pact. They delivered not only the wheat and
the oil for Hitler's war-machine, but also the propaganda
which could enflame the workers who forged the weapons
against Hitler's tyranny.

This extraordinary attack from the left fell on a stony
ground in England. The British workers, whom I began to
know well, appreciated all Haw-Haw appeals to sabotage, and
all Communist strike calls, as a big joke. Their ability to tame
the snake by the genuine reaction of hilarious laughter over a
pint of beer has never been interpreted as the spiritual asset
which it is. Just as Dante can descend to the lowest depth of
hell and survey the monsters of treachery, so, in 1940, the
workers could listen to conspiratorial threats and promises,
without being moved to respond, except by laughter.

I marvelled at this fearlessness and incorruptibility. How
was it possible for ordinary people to have this positive faith

and thus avoid being trapped by half-truths? I soon discovered that this state of grace was not religious. Overtly, at least, it had nothing to do with the Christian tradition. It sought no sacramental help nor revelatory sustenance. Yet it drew upon the same inner resources which Shakespeare's plays immortalized. These people were as pert and as innocent as Bottom and his friends in *A Midsummer Night's Dream*. One wondered if a Falstaff would abandon them on the field of battle? Would they still bleed to death while the fat knight would walk away, hale and hearty, with a cynical disquisition about 'honour'?

The 'people' now came into their own as far as I was concerned. They seemed to matter far more than even the cleverest theologies. During the dark evenings and on the rounds of civil defence one met endlessly and registered the total gulf between human reality and manuals, commentaries, edicts, and the like. Tolstoy's *War and Peace* came to my mental rescue. I was in the middle of it when the real war began on 10 May and the Germans broke through the lines in France, Holland, and Belgium after their complete victory in Norway. During the weeks and months of the imminent invasion and the bombing I prayed to be alive until I finished this book. The prayer was granted and the book came to fill the hole which the religious writers were then unable to fill. Tolstoy the genius had something to say about war which the prelates were too frightened even to raise as a question. They were lucky if they could shepherd their sheep by some dodge.

Tolstoy, by telling the story of human beings against the vast canvas of history, ended for me the terrible silence. His Prince Andrew, the Rostovs, Bezukov, Kutuzov, and the rest, articulated my own hopes and fears as the bombers appeared, first by day, and soon at night. His characters answered to the quest after such things as Providence in history, the place of suffering, religion, and virtue in the maelstrom of uncontrollable happenings. I saw a dogfight in the air and the crash of a Spitfire in conditions which evoked the words of the wounded Prince Andrew at Austerlitz: 'I had never seen it like this', referring to the utter peace of the sky and the lazy clouds trailing across. The whole novel had this quality of disclosing what one had always known and yet never apprehended. It did not make sense of the war and the bombs, but it gave one distance from it, even when the church and houses were on fire and the dead had to be carried out.

Religion came out very badly in *War and Peace*. This verdict agreed with my own experience that we were ascribing the oddest and most immoral events to the Almighty. After a night's bombing the lucky ones could be heard to say, perhaps for my benefit: 'God has been good to us', and I shrank from a sense of shame. Yet I had prayed to be allowed to live to read *War and Peace* and so felt implicated in this repulsive process of ejaculating hopes and fears. Tolstoy's vigorous honesty demolished credulity and superstition and even made nonsense of scriptural identifications. Peter Bezukov's childish dreams of being the killer of the Beast on the grounds of fitting letters and numbers belonged to a world of fantasy from which it was high time to wake up.

More seriously, however, Providence also fared badly under Tolstoy's treatment. Just because he gave full vent to the irresistible power of events and by belittling the importance of personal genius (Kutuzov is a good commander because he falls asleep and does next to nothing) Tolstoy did not so much deny Providence as the goodness of the predetermined course. Was this not a modern version of fatalism? In the tiresome epilogue of the novel he exposes himself and the reader to the full glare of a politico-military determinism in which neither God nor man play any part. It happens, that is all. The illiterate peasant soldier knows best. Napoleon is a mere accident; X could have done the same. But, as I saw it, Hitler and Churchill were not just X. Nor were we acting out a predetermined destiny.

But worst of all, the Peace which follows the War is a dénouement so boring that one may almost wish not to see it. In the novel the death of Prince Andrew marks the climax, and we know that Tolstoy himself got terribly bored with the sequel. Yet the sequel has the ring of truth about it. Thousands and thousands have died, but the survivors have learnt nothing. The domestic scene of anxious, dull, overworked mothers, children and babies with animal needs, and irritable men, explained in a way the madness of the human race, but it left a sour taste.

The miracle of the Battle of Britain countered the sceptical, and even gave a heroic, note to the resistance of the few to the many. We lived in this myth and were saved by it. After Dunkirk, and during the Battle of Britain, a return of religious confidence and spiritual awareness was unmistakable. The little boats had brought back hundreds of thousands from the beaches, the sea had remained calm without a ripple, the armada was repelled, and now 'Thank we all our God'. Churchill did not so much lead the praise but became the fulcrum of the national thanksgiving. Free from all show or transcendental rhetoric he became unwittingly a prophet in the hour of need. The great hymns — 'O God our help in ages past' — rang true, the churches were full. We were fighting not only for our lives, but for a cause which some would not hesitate to call sacred.

It is not often granted to men to live at a moment of history which they know to be decisive. June 1940 presented us with either life or death. I was prepared for the latter. The poison was well hidden and would be taken, for I was determined not to fall into the hands of the enemy. I anticipated then a decision which was ratified by many churches during the occupation, namely, that suicide could be not only permitted but regarded as a duty. This change of attitude, first adopted by Oates of Captain Scott's expedition in 1912, came to win acceptance, even in times of peace.

However, we were confident enought to opt for life. I was at King's College when all seemed lost and Pétain ready to sign the documents of defeat. Then Dean Hanson, most reticent of men, proclaimed again and again: 'They will not pass', and gave his philosophical reasoning for what was after all a highly improbable thesis. Soon after that a theological backing for godly resistance came from Switzerland. Karl Barth's famous, but then unexpected, call to Britain sustained the Christian conscience, weakened for years by superficial pacifist propaganda. In 1940 the Word of truth mattered, and his words had the ring of truth.

The 'finest hour' has turned out to have been just that. If one can assess the emotions, aspirations, and actions of a whole people at all, then this elusive concept England, Britain, the English, reached a high-water mark which, alas, also proved to be a watershed. To be alive in the winter of 1940—1 was certainly not heaven, but it was not hell either, despite the losses and the pain. A spiritual cohesion bound together a free community, and perhaps for the last time it achieved a balance of laughter and sorrow, tolerance and resolution, resistance and acceptance. The great spiritual heritage of prayer slotted into the fabric of such a people. It could even endure death without self-pity. But it always stopped short of a confessional Christianity. God, Christ, and the Holy Spirit may have been behind the 'finest hour', but the trinitarian face was obscured by the human.

I was, therefore, glad of the opportunity of broadening my own outlook by reading for a higher degree in the study of religions. My tutor taught me at Sion College on the Embankment. Once the place was on fire during a daylight raid, and he paid no attention until we had to move. My first enrichment came from him along unsuspected lines. He loved all animals and he assumed that no religious philosophy could be 'true' which did not make room for all creatures.

The comparative study of religions was then still in its infancy, though the great pioneers, who had collected the data in Asia and Africa, had left their mark earlier. But the fun of this study was perhaps the lack of professional expertise. You picked up the jewels from the trash. Best of all, you could still feel yourself to be an explorer. The vastness of Hinduism and Buddhism did not seem to be intimidating. You were free to mistake the less good for the fairest. For example, the *Bhagavad Gita* (since then often re-translated), which already ranked as the 'Song Celestial' in the West, stirred the newcomer with its hero Arjuna, the divine Krishna's charioteer. Here was a new voice which advocated responsible action and duty in the field. It offered universal salvation and confirmed the existence of an unchangeable order. The *Gita* helped me when I returned to the nights' alarms and the fearful sights in the mornings. Perhaps it was as well that I did not then know that this *Gita* holds a rather special place in the Scriptures which is not as high-ranking and representative of Hinduism as might be thought desirable.

Intense academic study provided me with an objective core and a wide horizon in the ever-tighter noose of wartime conditions. The Hindu edifice is not only endless but also rich in contradictions. After a sleepless night of bombs it is good to reflect that everything is, and that nothing is. Reality and illusion jostle each other agreeably. Again, to be drawn into a monistic system, and then turn the page to face a dualistic structure of the universe, was not only confusing but also true to experience. But perhaps the most notable find was the emphasis on the problem of suffering. Was suffering due to sin, or part of the human condition, or the illusory phantom which we can get rid of by wisdom and illumination? Could freedom from suffering be identified with a slipping away from identity, and did true bliss consist of the absorption of the self in non-being?

The questions could not be answered. It was enough for them to be raised, and I was happy to respond. Christians oddly place the suffering Christ in the centre of their icons, pictures, and music, but they cannot contain it in themselves. Many of us paid lip-service to the passion and death of Christ, and yet had never truly come to terms with a theology of the cross. The western affirmation of life, of the *élan vital*, proved too beguiling for us to accept its denial. However, I could not subscribe to the pessimism of the East, and especially the notion of the transmigration of the soul (if any) and reincarnation filled me less with dread than with an aversion to the absurd.

The course was so well structured that it balanced fantasy with scientific evaluation. Hitherto it had not occurred to me that science and religion had been uneasy bedfellows and that the rise of science was seen to contradict the claims of Christianity, not only in Communist countries but also in the West. Hence it was not only appropriate but necessary to explore this relationship. While Coventry was virtually wiped out by bombs I had the good fortune to study Leibniz's *Monadology*. The much-maligned genius, who could easily be derided for his doctrine of the 'best of all possible worlds' and 'the pre-established harmony', had a great deal to say in the light of modern mathematics and physics. It was a relief to turn from human phenomena and the human condition to the abstract world which simply could not be affected by the mess we made of ours. Here was a transcendence which was not prejudiced by concealed religiosity.

The war went badly, and the damage around one increased daily. A certain immunity to suffering was imparted to all. I visited hospitals and learnt the value of silent presence. Since my naturalization came through just in time I escaped internment and was not shipped to Canada on one of the fatal transports. Instead, I even visited army and air-force units and looked after Irish immigrants. Book-learning proved of no avail. Science was even less persuasive than religion.

An anti-intellectual tide engulfed me. My clients knew only the thirst of the appetites. Unlike Tolstoy's simple soldier they did not possess the natural insight ascribed to the untutored mind. They were stupid, and they wanted to remain stupid. In my impatience I failed to spot that they were frightened people who protected themselves with ignorance and indifference. What did gravitation, relativity, quantum physics mean to these bodies of interlocking molecules and chemical interactions? Yet if men were only atoms why did I, being atomic in structure, want to know the truth, not only about myself and other men, but about the laws of the universe? The apathy of my audiences intensified my search and I devoured books by Jeans and Eddington. *The Expanding Universe* was only a forerunner of the immense panorama which the cosmology of the next decades would bring to our notice, with big-bang and steady-state theories claiming our attention. It balanced for me that unsatisfactory task of learning about foreign gods and goddesses and the ways of the East. My tutor, whose passion for animals imparted to our tutorials under a sky filled with practising Flying Fortresses a contrasting serenity, rested his case for the gods on abstract ideas, whereas I pressed the claims of the galaxies as a guarantee of the eternal order.

The tide in the fortunes of war certainly affected our theological climate as a whole. Russia resisted the German invasion and the U.S.A. stemmed the Japanese advance in the Pacific. We were no longer alone. Our thinking also burst the conditions of siege. There was a distinct return to a cosmic Christianity in such English writing as could be published. The books emanating from this period prove the point. Above all, C.S. Lewis began to reach the public with his own version of the Divine Comedy. People were ready to open the windows to heaven and hell. Even in the Church the claustrophobic narrowness, along party lines, seemed to yield to an awareness of the eternal structures. The Church was no longer regarded as a parochial thing, an institution protected by the state, or even an agency for doing good. Lionel Thornton among many others saw the form of the Servant in the Church; the sacraments were not pious exercises on the part of individuals but the earthly re-enactment of the eternal pattern of creation and redemption. In prison camps, and even in the concentration camps which fed the extermination ovens, as well as in private studies and quiet libraries, men and women rediscovered the cosmic dimension, not as an intellectual luxury, but as the essence of humanity. Our hell was clearly the product of our unbelievable folly of considering man to be the measure of all things.

This turning towards a cosmic outlook proved fertile in the literary field, as the work of Charles Williams testifies. For the individual Christian, and specially the priest, with a parish such as Slough to contend with, such a cosmic stance in 1942 until the end of the war had its escapist ingredient. I installed a deck-chair at the back of old Upton church, on an ancient tombstone, basking in the peace around me. There were then no motorways; the alleged background to Gray's 'Elegy' could be savoured with an uninterrupted view to Windsor Castle and lyrical songs of birds and the lowing of the cattle. But I was not allowed to relax in pantheism. A beggar-priest, a little brother of Jesus, called Brother Edward, took me by the hand and with incomparable gentleness led me into his saintly realm of utter self-effacement. I had read about it in books, but this well-bred gentleman, turned ascetic village evangelist, opened the page of the simple communion with the living God. He was not learned nor capable of aesthetic enjoyment. He lived in prayer, for God and people. Suffering lined his thin, stern, loving face. He particularly loved, lived for, suffered on behalf of, the Jewish people. As if anticipating the news of the mass-killings he offered himself as the *Aqueda*, the bound sacrifice, Isaac at the hands of Abraham. He was entirely free from eccentric or neurotic self-assertion; rather the presence of the dying and risen Jesus radiated through his fragile frame. He would never bless me, but asked me to bless him. He gave by

81

receiving. The light shone out of his eyes, and when a few years later he lay dying I knew that the great intercessor, who had brought peace to all who touched him, would continue to intercede in eternity.

Brother Edward, who had found no rest in any religious community and was always on the move, as a vagabond of Christ, stands for a continuing tradition in England. In his own time he was not popular in the Church. His sermons were like the voice of God, authoritative, apocalyptic, clear and cool like the waters. He saw the end of the present era and did not pray for mitigation. He was only concerned with the life in the Spirit. But he could never be accused of fanaticism or rigorism, for he submitted to the yoke in perfect charity. He wanted no power for himself. In his way he invalidated all theological systems, since he demonstrated the all-sufficiency of discipleship. He agreed, with a smile, that he, tone-deaf as he was, would one day be blessed with musical understanding. His total concentration in God paired well with the cosmic unity.

Windsor Park was in those days an oasis of quiet, and I repaired often on my bicycle to the Saville Gardens. You climbed over a ladder into paradise. There were benches between the little streams and beds of flowers flanked the paths. In the spring the air was translucent. With Brother Edward behind me I could pray and bring the desolation of mankind into the Godhead. One day my meditations were interrupted: a man, tall and serious, accompanied a lady, short and vivacious. This was the Queen of England, accompanied by Sir Stafford Cripps. They stopped by my bench and asked me after my affairs. My clerical dress gave me credibility, and I ventured to ask them about their business. It turned out to be the scheme which later produced Cumberland Lodge, as a meeting place for all sorts of conferences on matters affecting public life, moral issues, and cultural progress. Cripps was not Churchill's favourite. He was a Christian socialist, and a puritan to boot. Austerity as a means of social equity and private perfection alienated him from many churchmen, but gained him also friends among the agnostics. He stood on the borders, and his influence could already be measured, even before the elections of 1945 swept him into power under the aegis of the

Labour victory. In his way he and his followers represented the prophetic hope.

Cripps's socialism was a curious blend of Christian asceticism and un-Christian egalitarianism. He had seen enough of the ways of Moscow to disdain Marxist-Leninist strategy, for he and his generation still observed a high code of morality. The roots of the Crippsian socialism were early English. This tree had grown out of levelling protestations, Puritan piety, personal idealism with admixtures of Catholic ritual and scientific utilitarianism. I always regarded the whole thing as a curious hybrid and doubted whether Christian utopia could be baptized into modern collectivism, just as some Roman emperors and bishops had baptized pagan institutions with more or less success. Cripps had a better chance of success than most because he knew that the city of this world operates by stimulating envy and false desires. He also had the support of an enlightened majority who identified Christian politics with fair dealings and austere measures. They pointed to the rationing system as if it were a religious sanction for all times. But when they extended this concept of fairness to the proposed welfare state, which was planned, even down to its financial details, by Lord Beveridge, I knew instinctively that this fairness must become the foulness of post-war England. The figures were no more absurd than the principles. Utopia had once again arrived to be revealed as a boring sham.

But these hopes and illusions, whether believed in or not, were yet far off in 1942. Much nearer my immediate concern was the problem of community. The war provided an unprecedented opportunity for the making of new communities. This was true of every regiment and ship, but it applied in a more interesting way to the many groups which came together for a variety of reasons. There were pacifists from conviction, partly religious, partly humanistic; there were non-combatants who were not fit to fight at all and had not passed their medicals, often to their own disappointment. Then refugees, especially women and children who had not been interned, were homeless. This flotsam and jetsam of humanity was often joined, or catered for, by a remarkable section of leaders. Some were clergymen or ministers, others laymen of Quaker conviction. Many a bearded Tolstoy appeared on the scene to lead a band of brothers, modelled after the Bruederhof from Swabia, who had been exiled or sought the freedom of the United States. All these people differed in their ideologies. They issued their own bulletins and gave a progress or regress report. Since most of these communities were rural and had some land, either on loan or as freehold, their outlook was governed by economic and cultural interests which did not reflect the exigencies of war. Skilled craftsmen, artists, engineers voiced their needs in a mixed society, which also made room for the unskilled and even illiterate.

One such community existed in Sussex, not far from Horsham, at Nuthurst. George Gibson, a priest from south London, had brought a nucleus of evacuees to a farm called Micklepage, and here a comedy of peace and war could be enacted far from the nightmare of bombs. In this microcosm of contrasting traditions and conflicting standards the Christian centre, symbolized by the delightful chapel in the barn, was supposed to bring unity and harmony. To a surprising degree this was achieved, though often at the expense of very long meetings, far into the night. The principle of unanimity operated pretty well, being sustained by the strong leadership and an invisible but real hierarchy. Revolts about duties occurred from time to time. Some of the cooks were incompetent. The indigenous Sussex workers shook their heads in astonishment when the farm was being mismanaged by these urban planners. For example, in our zeal we had planted a badly ploughed field of some ten acres with a crop of tomatoes. Though the weather was favourable in 1941 the wretched things suffered from the drought and lack of fertilizer, and we harvested a negligible crop of little green fruit. There were worse disasters to come. But the real crises were social. The Jewish mothers and children from Central Europe resented their isolation, and if the war in Russia had not then reached such a dramatic climax some of these formidable ladies would have become unmanageable. However the defence, first of Moscow, then of Leningrad, and later of Kursk and Stalingrad, provided them with militant enthusiasm.

A community cannot function unless it serves a common and identifiable purpose. Micklepage proved this truism with both comic and sad consequences. Laziness, as always, provoked the wrath of the industrious. The bees hated the drones. The mothers competed for their children in the distribution of food, clothes, and comforts. Here clashes were inevitable. The tigress looks after her own cub and regards the others as enemies. This problem defied not only solutions but even peaceable discussion. The chapel and the cross did not radiate their benign influence to these areas of instinctive behaviour.

It was in such states of explosive tension that the Visitor of the Community came into my orbit. Dr George Bell had already become famous as the Bishop of Chichester. He had helped refugees and was, in fact, responsible for the families who had descended upon Micklepage. They regarded him as perfect. They could not understand his Christian views and like children overestimated his power in the state. His advent filled everyone with expectation, and since I had never had the good fortune of a meeting I joined in the common emotion. Even the preparations were impressive. The barn was beautified, the paths cleared of weeds, the houses cleaned from top to bottom, and the reluctant cooks went to their task with a will.

Bishop Bell was given a triumphal entry, but his personality had nothing of the charismatic leader. Never has there been a more normal human being. What made him remarkable was the absence of eccentricity, let alone ecstasy. Just because he loved poetry and music he required no artificial stimulus from outside. By his goodness he defeated all those who wished to give a fascinating account of his character. Yet he achieved the almost impossible, namely, being disliked by quite a number of people. In the diocese of Chichester, as in London, there were not a few who opposed him. The reason was that he stood for a Christian line of faith and conduct which was to become normative after his death.

Bell's ordinariness and safe position in the established order enabled him to see the extraordinary and shoulder the unsafe, without at any time feeling the terror which falls on the unsheltered pioneers. He could afford to look outward because his inward self had no cause to be afraid. When I met him, I loved him, but I was instinctively aware of the secrets which he carried about him and of which he must be silent. He wanted to know — about the Nazis, Berlin, Jews, Christians — but he did not let anything be known. He made peace in the community just by his presence.

Bell had by this time already imprinted Christian institutions with the outgoing openness of his own person. He never left anything to chance, and he knew that continuity of purpose is at least as important as the original vision. Thus worship, unity, social justice, international co-operation, were branches on the tree of the Kingdom of God, which had to be cultivated responsibly. Conferences and reports were only a means to the end, and the end was conventionally religious, namely, God. But Bell, by being pressed into service, did not shirk the detailed working out. It was not enough to have all the right contacts with the right people abroad: he had to stand by those who resisted the great evil, and oppose those who betrayed the right. Bell re-enacted for the modern age what martyrdom had meant in the glorious past. He manifested that glory which the world crushes though it cannot live without it.

The story of Bell's fight against Hitler and the German Christians' corruption has often been told and will live in the annals of history. No hagiographical turn of phrase is needed. The whole issue was simply one of obedience to the gospel, and the Jews, through no fault or virtue of their own, were at the centre of it. Bell fought racism as a Christian — 'too little alive to the agonizing fact that we ourselves were deeply affected', as he later acknowledged.[1] Bell had stepped out of the protected area of privilege.

Bell saw that Christianity was 'in default'[2] and did not conceal his sense of failure when we surrounded him with gratitude. He certainly did not succeed in the rescue operation of millions of Jews nor in the preservation of open cities. He did not even carry his own people in accepting responsibility in the measure demanded by his conception of free will and grace. Towards the end of the war he could, like Moses, see the promised land, but there was no entry for him. The power which he needed was denied him. Yet I could never

[1] R.C.D. Jasper, *George Bell*, 1967, p.113.
[2] Ibid., p.140.

see Bell as a tragic figure. Not only did his blue eyes sparkle with good humour, but his own interpretation of the age was too practical to be tragic. That Hitler and Nazi deeds denied the Spirit was a fact for Bell, who affirmed the reality of the Spirit with his unwavering support for the weak. Bell, who could so easily have been duped by Nazi gestures or bribed by their blandishments before the war, or driven to despair by Headlam and his sympathizers, lived and worked as if no exterior forces could move him. Perhaps he was the last Christian bishop in England who combined all the privileges of the upper class with a classless identity of the pilgrim on the road to an unknowable and probably dreadful terminus.

Contra mundum! – Bell led a rational, moral, realistic fight with the world. He opposed persecution, bombing, war-trials, vindictive legislation, and thereby offended the vested interest of the civil and military institutions. He may have been wrong in isolated instances (the use of the atom bomb?) but he saw to it that the end of the conflict in Europe was not without hope. The physical destruction was not matched by a spiritual capitulation to evil. On the contrary, as the crowds surged forward to shout and clap, to acclaim Churchill and then vote him out of office, and as the dreary aftermath of the war followed, with the opening of the tombs in Europe and the showing of horror upon horror, as the guilty were arraigned and, with few exceptions, defied in spirit the laws which they had already outraged, as the names of Bonhoeffer and many martyrs (Schneider, Metzger, Anne Frank) stood above the lists of millions of victims, we could make ready for a future, for we had been given a spiritual life in the process of dying around us. Perhaps never before in history has there been a more intense awareness of dying and rising.

11

UNSETTLED ACCOUNTS

I attended a music school at Down House in Berkshire and we were rehearsing Haydn's 'London' Symphony when the director interrupted the surging finale to announce that the atom bomb had been exploded over Hiroshima. No one said a word. Nagasaki became the twin of formerly unknown names who stood for the climax of the war in the Far East. Japan was beaten, the war finally ended in 1945, and once again we celebrated victory, possibly in a more muted key. Walking in the grounds of the school we concluded that nothing would ever be the same again. But how was one to interpret the unprecedented for oneself? Here opinions varied from the start. Miss Willis, the remarkable Quaker headmistress of the school, preached the sermon on that memorable Sunday morning. She stressed penitence and responsibility as the main ingredients of our future, but, on emerging from the chapel, I listened to discordant voices which expressed the opposite. Having reached such a pass, when we had the means of killing thousands — and, to be sure, millions in the near future — let us eat and drink in the present. These cynics were in their turn assailed by such humanists as claimed that now at last we had reached the turning-point in human affairs. War could never happen again. A world-wide community would surrender national ambitions and social justice would ensue on an international basis. San Francisco beckoned to the United Nations, sadly without Roosevelt, to open the grand formalities.

I listened to my fellow fiddlers and noticed that they were not disposed to hear me, for they knew that I was a Christian priest. From now on the humanists, however divided in their aims, eschewed their second place in English society. They were the teachers and not to be taught. Had not our Christianity led the world to the precipice? The war was over, but only thanks to our technical and moral superiority.

Prayers and the like had contributed nothing. The future would not be obscured by superstition but guaranteed by rational progress. When I pleaded with them and made much of the Christian doctrine of grace we reached the crux of the matter. They chided me for medieval credulity (was Augustine medieval?, I protested) and I countered by invoking their dedication to music. How could they account for Mozart, for example? As I brought out of my armoury the treasures of the past I silenced a few and we met on an aesthetic compromise. Perhaps music alone could top our atomic prospects.

Never shall I forget these evenings when the music ended and one could walk in the grounds. My private life was also shattered. I had played with the notion of a monkish existence, and as long as the war lasted Lady Poverty, Master Chastity, and even Lord Obedience could be served with equanimity. I had married others, whose prospects often ended in death in battle or presently in divorce after battle, and had no desire to follow their example. But now the soft nights beguiled me too. An overwhelming passion arose in me, and I came to realize that I had never truly lived. I had bestowed love on religion, and with the declaration of peace the old feeling receded. I would not contemplate the churchy life, unmarried, tied to my mother, without anything or anybody to call my own. Thus peace brought war within most unexpectedly.

In peacetime individual destinies, released from the grip of wartime duties, assert their claims. We were not prepared for this great change, which struggled in the British Isles against a more severe austerity than we had known before. Practical problems now engaged everyone's attention. Men and women were demobilized and though they returned to civilian life with apparent ease they lost the sense of solidarity. I realized that freedom really is a delicate plant and has to be nourished by material goods. Suddenly we were all in a hurry to find a better life, and the general devastation made it harsher instead. Others seemed to flourish, and these 'others' were envied. The seed of envy, which cannot germinate in war, fell on a welcoming ground. As a priest I noticed that the security from bombs had opened the insecurity of tombs within, but I had not yet grasped that there were unsettled accounts far more serious than the little bickerings over rations and housing.

On the Continent the reunion of families took much longer or did not follow at all. My mother and I were daily expecting to hear of my father, last heard of in Holland in 1941. The radio stations broadcast the names of wives searching for their husbands, and I listened to the Dutch and the French bulletins. The lists seemed endless. Parents searched for their children, and orphans suddenly found that father or mother, or both, were still alive and they were children once again, in a family, under one roof, scarred with wounds, but miraculously preserved. Yet only too frequently they remained alone, and there was no response from the still wastes in the East. I went to the Red Cross and filled in forms, and even included my brother's name, last heard of in Russia in 1937.

Gradually the truth came to us, just as one assembles a jig-saw puzzle. The final picture resembles a nightmare and could not be accepted. Only when I saw the first documentary film, made by the British, of the concentration camp of Belsen (some said it should never have been shown) could the eyes command the mind to register the extent of the killing. I had ministered to the dying and I had officiated at funerals, but I had never contemplated mountains of bones, skulls, legs, arms. I had seen Goya's 'Horrors of War' and also the medieval chapels with skulls, but here was no painting nor a cautionary symbol. Corpses lay upon corpses, and we were still spared the stink of decomposition.

The unimaginable forced upon our minds yet worse. I had been fed upon the notion, now found illusory, that pain has its limits. C.S. Lewis, for example, had said that the quantity of suffering could not increase its quality. Christians believed that one cross and crucifixion contained the sum-total of human degradation. But, alas, this turned out to be false as one Belsen was followed by another Buchenwald, and soon the whole map of eastern Europe was seen to be dotted with extermination camps. The Jewish people could now be seen to be the entombment of all mankind. But were these millions of murdered innocents — the final figure has never been computed — meaningless victims? If they died in vain how could one speak of the tragedy of the Jewish people? And if they were not redeemed and reconciled, in and after death, how could there be any hope for mankind, even if the war was now won and some of the cruel criminals set at nought?

Auschwitz became the massive symbol of the enduring stain of mankind. At the end of 1945 it became plain that my father had also been gassed there. He had been arrested in Holland, transported to Theresienstadt, and finally taken to the station from which there was no return. A few of his works came over later from Amsterdam, among them a score of Mozart's *Idomeneo*. which I still have. The lines 'Figlio, perdona' are underlined, as if I had anything to forgive. Did my father suffer greatly, or did Bach's entreaty 'when we are in direst need' entirely possess his spirit, so that music flooded him beyond the torture of existence?

Of my brother we never heard again. Since 1945 millions of words, pages of pictures, annals of documentation, and personal statements have appeared and are now safely shelved in libraries to plead against the unspeakable evil of our time. But the accounts remain open, unsettled, unbalanced. The facts were tried during the trials of the war criminals, but these were never interpreted, since no court of law can examine and sentence the motivation of criminals whose defence monotonously intones: 'I acted under orders'. The final solution, they claimed, came out of devotion to duty and blind obedience. Such pleas were not then accepted, but they prevented a further probing into the hearts of the men, who, according to their memoirs, loved their families and gardens during the years of genocide.

The victims, too, left open accounts, though not of guilt or compliance. Only a few left voices for the future. Such a one was Edith Stein, the Jewish Carmelite nun, who accepted death as martyrdom and achieved the miracle of forgiveness. Another figure, more famous and for years a goal of young pilgrims, was Anne Frank, whose *Diary* swept the world in the fifties and described the anguish of concealment, the empty hope for a future, and the need to love and be loved against a background of irritation, fear, and the threat of annihilation.

One victim who survived was the Rabbi Leo Baeck, who was to join a theological society to which I also belonged. In Theresienstadt he had fulfilled a ministry which Christians would have called priestly. Among the dying and those destined to die he had maintained the order of the law of God, the tradition of civilized humanity, the genuine hope of the kingdom of righteousness which kindles the hearts of the despairing. Baeck lived in England for part of the time and spoke to us on problems of faith. He never referred to his own exploits nor to the crimes which he had witnessed. It was known that he had interceded for the murderers at the hour of liberation, but he rejected for himself the aureole of sanctity. I wondered whether Baeck could be said to balance these unsettled accounts, but I could come to no conclusion. Alas, the huge debt stood in no relation to any personal merit; it must always outweigh the bravery of the few and the virtue of the elect. The Auschwitz machine and its operators stood outside the circle of redemption. I could, therefore, hardly sympathize with the new and aggressive views of post-war Christians, who ignored the unredeemed past and moralized happily for the present, as if men could just top their natural wickedness with a dressing of good will. Strangely enough, Baeck himself could be misunderstood as a good German liberal, who mixed Goethe with enlightened Jewishness to yield an attractive, but ineffective ethics.

However, effective aid was needed for the survivors, and the Jewish–Christian ethic proved its efficacy in a thousand ways. Long words, such as reconciliation and forgiveness, were given flesh by those who had smelt the stench of Belsen. Victor Gollancz came to typify the Jew who burst Judaism, and the Christian who went back to the heart of Jesus, in order to transcend the loathing one felt for the defeated Germans. I had always liked him as a left-wing publisher and a religious heretic who believed in the living God. But I had also suspected his mixture of sentimental zeal and commercial shrewdness. These suspicions vanished when I realized that he pinpointed the act of forgiveness as the concrete moment in space, when God acts in us or we act for God. Instead of making a cult of the disgust, which fuels feelings of revenge. Gollancz clearly suppressed his own emotions before he embarked on his 'Save Europe Now' campaign, which in the black years of total ruin repeated the feeding which had kept me alive in 1923. In his religious anthologies Gollancz was to show that he knew better than most that all humanitarian deeds can but serve as faint copies of the perfect truth. But at least they demonstrate that sacred texts can be rewritten in the bodies disfigured by hunger and guilt. 'Save Europe Now' became more than a slogan for me, for it articulated the whole post-war problem of corporate guilt, individual destiny, and the religious affirmations of the past. How was one to make sense of all that had been lost?

The problem touches the deep, and in 1945 it spoke through and to aching hearts. Some prophetic voices had been stilled by friendly death. William Temple, for example, had, like Roosevelt, died before the victory. They had crowned their years with success and were no cause for tears. But Bonhoeffer had been hanged by his captors on 9 April 1945, only a few weeks before the Nazi surrender. Bethge, his friend, has left to us a monumental biography which allows us to fill in all the details of the last years and days. But when we heard of Dietrich's death in 1945 we still groped in the dark and could hardly hope that any of his friends had been spared. We mourned for him and for his family, especially for his fiancée, who embodied all the shattered hopes of their own future. I responded then, and have never ceased to do so, with the recitation of the laments in the Bible and in the tragic poetry, classical and modern. Bonhoeffer's death, though entirely achieved in our century and with cool deliberation, struck the ancient, timeless cord, the *De profundis*, the 'Man that is born of woman has but a short time to live'. Dietrich was to become the catalyst of Christian existence in the days to come, but his writings could have availed nothing if they had not been authenticated by his resistance to the tyrant and submission to our tragic destiny, the gallows.

Who then is guilty? Our modern tragedy could not accommodate guilt, nor provide reconciliation, as the great classical tradition had done. Our Furies would not settle down at the hearth but remained hell-bent on vengeance and further destruction. The ordinary layman, however, wished to ignore the whole sordid mess and leave it to the international court at Nuremberg to punish the guilty. Only one of the major war criminals pleaded guilty. This man, Frank, ex-Governor of Poland, had become a Christian and acknowledged his share in the vast organization of murder. His former colleagues coolly repudiated their guilt and felt no remorse. I read the proceedings and have re-read volumes of transcripts of later trials and have not been able to still my despair. Mountains of guilt, already piled high from past centuries, reach up from this earth, unatoned, unrepented, and ever-active in the huge pollution of this planet.

Yet the reaction to this spiritual aftermath of the war was negligible. There were, of course, memorial services. Bell, for example, spoke in honour of Bonhoeffer. But the churches were exhausted and had to forget the past in order to deal with the present. Their internal troubles were bad enough and the programmes of rebuilding absorbed time and money. The English churches proceeded as if the crop of the grapes of wrath could be forgotten.

The German Protestants, under their bishops (Lilje and Wurm being prominent), met to come to terms with the crimes committed in their name. They faced the insoluble problem of corporate guilt and signed the Declaration of Guilt in Stuttgart in October 1945. It remains one of the few documents to review the infernal past in the light of Christian belief. Bell was present at its ratification and responded to the confession, which does not set out to be a political confession of collective guilt but rather a spiritual clarification. Even so it shocked many Germans at the time. For me it did not go nearly far enough. I was also highly disturbed by its even tenor and the vagueness of its clauses, which seemed to me highly inappropriate, seeing that the crimes committed had not suffered from any vagueness whatsoever. Even now in retrospect the tone sounds too general and pious. The Evangelical Church addressed the ecumenical community under five headings: (1) Acknowledgment of guilt — 'we accuse ourselves of not having confessed more courageously, prayed more faithfully, believed more cheerfully, loved more fervently'; (2) A new beginning is to be made; (3) Gratitude is offered for the ecumenical community; (4) The spirit of force and revenge is to be replaced by common service; (5) Invocation of the Holy Spirit for the whole of Christendom.

It will be noticed what the Declaration did not state. It skated over the real heart of the matter, namely, that the Church had not rescued the persecuted, nor supported the individuals who had taken great risks in helping them to escape; that the Church had lent no support to the conspirators against Hitler and left Bonhoeffer to his fate; that they had failed to denounce the murderers from the start and had misjudged the regime before and after 1933. The umbrella of general penitence obscured these issues. On the other hand it helped to prepare the ground for the making of restitution to the survivors of the victims and to clear the air for reconstruction in Germany.

The reason for this reticence in the acknowledgement of guilt is not far to seek. The churches merely represented the feeling of their own congregations. Families craved for sympathy instead of offering repentance. They, too, had suffered grievously. We suffer from self-pity, when we have lost homes and loved ones. When all have suffered there remains little room for fine distinctions of guilt. As I looked at the pictures of dead soldiers in Austrian cemeteries and the widows and children at Mass I sensed a tearfulness of things which defied consolation. Forgiveness, like repentance, had become far too rare a virtue to appease and heal the outraged. Mass murder and anonymous slaughter fitted into no Christian framework.

The Catholic Church never even went so far as to make a nominal resolution or to call for restitution. Here the past soon merged into the terrible present, when eastern Europe came under the heel of the Red Army. In the West the goodwill for the Soviet forces still lingered and we could not grasp the nature of the Russian attacks. Stalin's so-called intransigence came to help the West at length when Marshall Aid saved western Europe from total chaos and the centre of gravity shifted to America. I shared in the ensuing confusion of mind. During the war the successes of the armies of Zhukov, Koniev, Rokossovsky, had filled our drooping spirits with enthusiasm. They had liberated the death camps in the east. When crews returned from Soviet ports and told of the terror, when displaced persons arrived from behind the Iron Curtain (a phrase which Churchill coined on 18 August 1945), one pushed their undesired reports away in order to cling to the belief in the Great Alliance. The wilful blindness of 1933 was upon us again, and I was tempted by the sin which I had decried in others. I was only alerted to the Marxist fraud when the party line decreed that the Jewish holocaust must be explained by dialectical materialism. Capitalists, which included Jewish entrepreneurs and monopolists, had been guilty, not in terms of sin but of class structure, just as the bourgeois class was now preventing working-class justice, unless overcome by Red Army intervention. I listened to the smooth and endlessly repeated talk, called dialectic, and I threw off the romantic mantle of socialist pretensions.

As at the time of Munich in 1938 I had reached a turning-point. Though the world was for ever stained and the stench of the air could not be purified by illusions I had decided to live and not to die. I could not now be fobbed off with pious platitudes nor with Marxist analyses. I could not solve the problem of guilt in the manner of psycho-analysis, nor follow the liberal obfuscation and blur moral distinctions by asserting: 'We are all guilty, and there but for the grace of God go I', pointing to Hitler's gang now facing execution. I knew the facts by day and suffered from the shadows at night. But I returned to the quest after God, freed from parochial concerns and in the setting up of a faculty of theology, newly constituted at King's College, London. We still addressed God as God and proclaimed the knowledge and love of God. How could this be?

Our resilience must startle the observer from outer space. In our struggle to live we seek movement, and new places seem to wash away our pollutions. In 1946 I crossed the Channel, for the first time again since the war. Bell happened to be on the same boat — a good omen. After eighteen hours across France the train arrived in Basel. The walk from the dark, dirty French station, through the controls, to the Swiss building symbolized the resurrection from death. Here was light, food, cleanliness, normality, despite strict rationing. I descended to the Rhine, pulled off my shoes, stood in the clear moving water, looked up to the Minster in golden sunshine, and felt rebaptized for life.

Throughout this decade and later Basel became more than a reminder of better times. It drew theological and philosophical pilgrims and the university was the Mecca. Barth and Jaspers taught here. Their interpretation of our past was not history in retrospect, but the linking of this history with the immutable truth. Barth's *Dogmatic Theology* had grown during the siege of war into what was to become the greatest monument to theology in the twentieth century. The war and its aftermath delayed the English translation, and there remained a time-lag until the author's death in 1968. Barth, the pillar of the theological resistance, the academic, the preacher, the prison visitor, the gracious host, the helper of students, lover of Mozart, succeeded in the difficult art of not becoming a legend in his lifetime. He really lived and worked in Basel. He could be heard and read, questioned and opposed. He had no school and desired none. He abstained from seeking publicity and was not taken in by stunts of any kind. Jaspers, a medical doctor by training, versed in psychiatry, fugitive from Heidelberg with a Jewish wife, was a genius of a very different kind. He could claim to be representative of a post-war world which questioned existence itself and struggled to give an existential answer to the possibility of non-being. Those who listened to Barth and Jaspers were sandwiched between two irreconcilable spheres of faith, and this tension agreed with one's experience.

Not that experience mattered to Barth! Indeed, the main thrust of his work went right against English pragmatism. Religious experience, in his eyes, was as worthless as a guide to truth, as the lack of religious experience. Barth put the world upside down. But whereas in *The Epistle to the Romans* his tone had been rhetorical, paradoxical, and provocative, he now eschewed the dramatic style. Neither Kierkegaard nor Dostoyevsky accompanied the mature Barth. In careful and elaborate exposition, Barth drew upon the rich past and thence confronted the present. He answered to my despair not by answering it but by refusing to admit the type of

questioning which most of us indulged in. The world made
no sense, the outrages of the war cried to heaven, the facts
did not add up to any kind of faith: very well, agreed Barth,
this is part of the gospel before the gospel, namely, the
realization that the world is god-less, and that you as part of
it, cannot know God. Without hysterics and shrieks of anguish
he stated once again the infinite qualitative distinction
between God and man, the apophatic tradition of the Orthodox Church, the *via negativa* of the Latin Church: God is
invisible, unknowable, incomprehensible. Thus man's only
worth-while search for God lies in its failure, the realization
that it gets nowhere. Out of this scepticism alone comes
the disclosure of the gracious God, who, through his Word,
written, proclaimed, in our midst, also shows himself to be
our God, the Lord for us.

Now all this had been said before, and Barth never disguised his debt to tradition. To the surprise of most, this
very unecclesiastical theologian insisted on calling his theology
a *Church* dogmatics. It was not churchy, but it did not
freewheel privately. It sprang out of the community of faith
and was addressed to it. Barth had to assume, for example,
the authority of the Bible. Yet he did not speak as a literalist
and nothing was more foreign to him than fundamentalist,
right-wing, conservative ideology. His Bible was not a closed
book, but the speech of and about the Christ, Jesus of
Nazareth. In short, there was no general theology, no ecumenical lowest common denominator, no sectarian privilege,
but only the self-revealing God in Christ by the Holy Spirit.

This theocentric stance, once accepted, was not silent in
our world. We could see ourselves, in time and space, through
Jesus Christ, elected, sanctified, justified, accepted, loved.
In obedience to his for-us we became to-him the sons, the
dying and rising people of God. Barth could not help becoming
more and more joyful in the factual exploration of the
hidden become revealed, for he had entirely broken with the
straining after evidence and the paragraphing of duties.

Barth gave me breathing space. The oppression yielded
because in his perspective the eternal not only contained,
but also controlled, the temporal. God himself settled our
accounts in our universal state of bankruptcy. Even the

'facts' of history, the rotting skeletons, the gassed children, the barbed wire, the searchlights and the towers, were no longer facts but rather 'non-facts', exposed in their emptiness through the person and work of Christ. I did not subscribe to the view that Barth indulged in a ludicrous optimism, or in a Gnostic disregard of historical facts, since I admired his insistence that it was the crucified Christ who held and holds the orb and the sceptre against the hostile world. He also saw the plight of the Jews not as a historical disturbance but, in the light of Romans 9-11, as part of the providential 'for us' order. Faith could make sense even of Judas. Back in England, where Barth was not greatly liked and his theology held to be unreadable and too long, if not downright irresponsible and unethical, doubts returned. Could it be that Barth's restatement of the old Protestant *Sola Fide, Sola Gratia*, was too good to be true? Or was this faith so good because it was true?

Jaspers's 'philosophical faith' had nothing in common with Barth's Christocentric theology. It confirmed one's sceptical evaluation of history and institutions. Yet Jaspers also refused to bow to things as they appeared. We must 'penetrate the phenomena', he insisted. The aim, the truly human achievement, is not to accept objective and historical facts but to transcend them. We cease to be spectators and in any case never are spectators if we live at all. Language which communicates and liberates opens up the perspectives of real existence. Christ and the Trinity are not negligible ciphers in this language, but they are by no means the only ones. Moreover, they are not free from absurdity and even 'block the way which the relation to Transcendence shows us'.[1] Indeed, recalling Kant's *opus posthumum*, Jaspers exposes the whole weakness of theological objective claims: 'God is my own thought, not a thing extant outside me.' Therefore it is pointless to ask whether God 'is'.

Jaspers and all the existentialists so-called (Sartre, Heidegger, Camus, Marcel) had one thing in common which not only appealed to me, but seemed to be cogently true: the world of phenomena and of history defeated us, unless we took it by

---

[1] *Philosophical Faith and Revelation*, London 1967, pp.166ff.

its throat and imposed an order on it, by which we transcended both it and ourselves. There was something naive about the attempt, but these men of genius made it look and feel less naive. Jaspers in particular made it quite clear that to be existentialist need not land one up in a lunatic asylum, dreaming that one is Napoleon or Hitler. On the contrary, all existentialists aimed at healing the wound of madness. They focused upon the experiences of the immediate past, especially of the occupation of France. Then the Maquis had been faced with the razor's edge form of existence: 'To be or not to be' ceased to be a quotation from Hamlet.

Jaspers took one to the heart of the problem of existing in an absurd world. He relieved the sense of anguish by placing this absurdity not only in history, but also in man's philosophical countering of absurdity in history. The past, though viewed critically, was by no means dead. Thus existentialism was freed from its own absurdity, namely, the notion that the decision which you make here and now is the only thing that matters. Unfortunately, the vulgar use made of existentialism led to the popularization of a few clichés, and the talk about 'commitment', 'involvement', 'decision', 'freedom', 'transcendence' yielded a string of rhetoric without much meaning. This abuse parodied 'existence' and made Kierkegaard, the implacable enemy of all 'isms and generalizations, look silly.

Whenever I visited Basel I hovered between Barth and Jaspers and tested their theses against my own experiences in England. Jaspers's self-transcendence seemed then a weak plant in English soil and made me agree with Barth's verdict: 'empty, barren, and at bottom profoundly dull'.[1] Our grey post-war reality, in which a Labour administration restricted freedom, simply lacked any sign of a transcendent reference. The spokesmen from the Left advanced without a hint of transcendence. No, existentialist claims, I inferred, could only affect the individual. But even this option lacked strength, for where is the individual who can carry the whole world on his own? The ancient myths spelt out a warning, for was not Atlas punished by Zeus by having to

---

[1] Jaspers, op.cit., pp.326ff, for the still fascinating debate.

support the pillars of the universe, and was not his brother Prometheus chained to the rock? Soon enough the vultures would come and pick the Promethean individual's liver.

However, perhaps this was not the correct analysis. From France came the authentic voice of rebellion against authority. Sartre and Camus had lived through the war and now articulated the nausea of living in a world of enemies. Freedom was offered in action, and such action must often be directed against one's neighbours. This made sense even in England, where the sights were lowered and the rhetoric of destruction lost its nastiness. The Outsider became an engaging figure, who combined 'being and doing' against a background of endless officialdom and form-filling.[1] But Christians did not feel as outsiders yet and gave a cool response to existentialism.

I enjoyed the pincer movement of Barth's dogmatic faith, God's own revelation, and the existentialist work from below which identified freedom with action. At last I felt strength enough to rise above the past and to ignore the threats of the present. But words would remain words unless they took flight. Prayer may be cocooned in words, and decisions may be couched in words, and this sterility of words hung heavily upon my soul. Music, it is true, frees words from their rational base, and the discovery of Beethoven's quartets opened a new spiritual dimension which superseded words. But it vetoed my single life and my determination to be alone, without risks and entanglements. I disliked the Anglican type of celibacy around me, which was precious and playing life as a game. I prayed for a wife, a companion, a friend, a love to whom I could bring not only ideas, aims, and promises, but myself. A new account opened after a chance meeting of egregious boredom where educational matters were being discussed and formulated in the new style of administrative jargon. She sat at the far end of the table, smoking and unhappy. I ambushed her on the way out. She refused an invitation to a Beethoven concert in view of a promise given beforehand to see a student. I was angered, then sensed fidelity. We became engaged, had our first

---

[1] Cf. Colin Wilson's *The Outsider*, 1956.

quarrel, were reconciled, and were married. All our friends came to the ceremony at Westminster Abbey, in whose precincts she had been born. The sermon was truly theological and enunciated matters of life and death, past tragedies and future consummation.

Marriage balanced old accounts of despair and opened new ones of contradictions. Despite the mystical halo, lingering over from the church ceremony, I discovered that this sacrament reflected all the tensions between heaven and earth. On the one hand the likeness to Christ's love for his Church transfigured our attachment to a celestial union, as if we were already Dante and Beatrice, and on the other hand the search for a home, the rebuffs by estate agents, the squabbles over electricity bills with our priestly landlord, reminded us that we were truly on earth. But more alarming were the inner contradictions, when the joys of fleshly union revealed a vast range of varying, even negative, responses. The simplest needs stood in conflict with the complex scenario. Old friends had to be dispatched lest they come between man and wife. Parental devotion turned to interference which had to be opposed. Within the narrow compass of marriage I experienced the pressures of our external history. The arrival of children changed my whole scale of values. Suddenly the important events seemed trivial, for who cares about the rape of a country when a baby at home is on the point of death? Or who can rejoice over a better trade balance when a child first puts his hand into that of his father to go for a walk, and intimates to him the trust that Jesus talks about? Children educate their parents, especially in humility, as when a youngster protests indignantly: 'you think yourself so wonderful', thus demolishing the *hubris* of our personal history.

As I ceased to look at things from the outside and experienced the endless refractions of energy from within a shared life, I learnt that our earthly accounts can never be squared. Since it is impossible to quantify the dimensions of love in their infinite variety it must be equally beyond us to get the dimensions of hatred right in our books. Bookkeeping comes to an end when we are sandwiched between the ecstasies and miseries of the private life, on the one hand,

and the contingencies of an uncontrollable world on the other. I profited from a stay in hospital with an undiagnosed illness which symbolized for me the immeasurable ways in which the sick, their dependants, the staff, and the machines interact apart from, and yet always dependent upon, the huge immensity outside. I concluded that one is coerced to do justice to both ends of the spectrum: the little world of one's own, the *microcosmos* of love, its joys and failures; and the *macrocosmos*, the unknown which dauntingly spells out the future. As the jubilee year of 1950 came round I had ascended another twist of the spiral staircase which leads to this unknown. Now I had under me the sure foundation of a home.

12

UNFORESEEN CHANGES

Words, words, words! I look back with amazement at millions of words in books, magazines, pamphlets, reports, letters, briefs, broadcasts, year by year, month by month, week by week, day by day. We have invented, and bowed to, a mythology of our own making. And yet, out of this welter and above the morass, there is the Word, the eternal Logos, diffused into scriptures, broken into tongues, transmuted in recital and in writing, taken up by new minds and pens, interpreted and interpreting, in endless forms, with manifold aims, returning a spiritual harvest. I stand apart, at a distance, a responsible family man, and survey the past, the decade of the fifties, which now seems so remote, far more distant than the age of Isaiah or Pericles. It does not look a good period in retrospect and the question, always uppermost in my mind, nags and torments: why did it have to be thus? Why did we not order our lives differently after the great holocaust? Have we no freedom, despite all the talk, the words, words, words? Could we have foreseen the changes and altered the direction of our affairs? And if we did not, who is accountable? How is it possible that so much ink has been spilt for so little purpose? Does energy simply obey its own impetus and thus change our conditions, and ourselves, at random?

This predicament did not disturb the world at the time. Things happened: Eastern Europe came wholly under the heel of Russia, except Yugoslavia under Tito. Stalin died and after a tussle Khrushchev ruled. The Korean war ended in stalemate. Eisenhower's peaceful reign began. The British retreat from empire began and proceeded without troubling public feeling. A Festival of Britain in 1951 and the mourning for King George VI in 1952 marked the transition. The accession of the young Queen heralded the new era in which Britain declined and Germany recovered miraculously, through hard work, from the ruins. Though the ration-book and the queue gradually disappeared and the black market ceased to operate British solidarity gave way to party faction. A vacuum yawned behind the desire for fairness and equality. The theological scene was calm to the point of being colourless. There might have been no war. No great changes were envisaged. Pacifist Christians campaigned against nuclear arms and the time-honoured call for good works evoked still responses of the *de haut en bas* (paternalistic) type. A mission to London spurred the clergy and their followers to an ephemeral wave of enthusiasm. Even the recruitment of missionaries for work overseas still flourished. I remember a meeting in the Albert Hall where thousands acclaimed the call 'China for Christ' with money and men. Our expectations were immoderate though our mental resources had been run down.

Sometimes you light a fire in the garden and next morning the embers are still aglow, and much later you find that wild flowers spring up around it. Our theological enterprise resembled such an afterglow or unexpected bloom. The students had found their vocation in the crucible of conflict. Some, as soldiers, sailors, and airmen, had come through the fire and often fulfilled a vow in offering themselves for the ministry. Now they were prepared to go back to school. They had to re-learn Latin, and start New Testament Greek and Hebrew from scratch. Books were a source of worry rather than delight after years of service in the forces. They were disciplined in prayer and rose early for mass and practised meditation. Yet they never aspired to high aims, such as mystical contemplation. They played as they prayed, football in the winter, and cricket in the summer. They never indulged in wartime nostalgia and disregarded rumours of new wars. Their teachers spurned excitement and new doctrines. The emphasis was still on historical and comparative studies, always on the supposition that given diligence and good will the truth was available and acceptable. Professor E.O. James, for example, combined a liberal wisdom with a Catholic devotion, undeterred by his archaeological digs and recent finds in the Middle East. The facts pointed to God. The classical ways of demonstrating God's existence from motion, causality, contingency, multiplicity seemed unquestioningly right. The unmoved Mover and necessary Being could be detected as ever in the design of the world and the purpose of every creature.

This mirage of a return to the antique faith possessed also the churches, as they repaired their buildings with the aid of war-damage payments. Only the organization had to be streamlined to conform to the new demands. Benefices were united and some churches had to close. But these were local issues. The former entrenched positions between Catholics and Protestants lost none of their vigour. In America, to be sure, the tension between parties, sects, and movements reached unprecedented sharpness.

Happy were these days and deceitful in their effect. The churches scored triumphs in their relief of hunger, the settling of refugees, and in a vast educational expansion. A boom in religious literature fed an apparently endless demand for information. The appearance of new periodicals, monographs, dictionaries, lexica, commentaries, texts, and translations, the enthusiasm for biblical studies in learned societies, found a suitable climax in the finds in the Judaean desert and in Egypt. I joined the rush of researchers in the promised land which flowed with the milk of new evidences and the honey of comparative data. I forgot about the crisis of mankind and after a *Theology of Crisis*, published in 1948, I turned the wheel of my craft and wrote a *Theology of Salvation*. It was a good time and accordingly I explored the Christian tradition of heaven and our ascent to bliss.

Christian triumphalism was no academic exercise or empty propaganda. The Jubilee Year of 1950 had reached heights of glory visible and audible in Rome and at Fatima. Despite the aftermath of war Pope Pius XII headed the Curia in the celebrations. I was among the countless pilgrims who flocked to the scene of the militant faith triumphant without weapons. We united our trust in the intercessory power of the Blessed Virgin Mary, whose Corporeal Assumption became the source of joy and comfort to millions. The Pope ratified the dogma in defiance of the world which erred and sinned and persecuted. The rumours of his mystical visions enhanced his aristocratic dignity, a true prince of the Church, a shepherd in the endless hierarchy. Only a few years would pass and one would hear veiled, and then open, accusations against the same man. He died before Hochhuth and others made him the scapegoat of Catholic arrogance and indifference to wartime pogroms and genocide. Who could have thought under the Roman sky, on the Aventine hill in the balmy air of the night, that the ruler of spiritual Rome, who had opened his Vatican fortress (such as it was) to a number of Jewish fugitives, would come under the condemnation of the new generation of journalists, playwrights, scriptwriters, and publicity-seeking communicators?

Such changes were not yet foreseen. The Christian triumphalism spilt over into the world beyond the confines of ecclesiastical institutions. Not only new monastic enterprises flourished, especially in America where some of the finest houses were now built, but the political regimes in Europe consolidated the feeling of a Christian continent. Adenauer's West Germany and de Gaspari's Italy paved the way to the concept of the United States of Europe. In Zürich Winston Churchill endorsed the hope of millions, and Strasbourg became the centre of the spirit of reconciliation. I attended a conference there and noticed the eagerness with which former enemies shook hands and new friendships were made. Christians of all denominations, Jews, and unbelievers, forged their solidarity in the world of learning. I was moved by one example, however trivial by itself: Professor Hempel had been an officer in the S.S. and his record had been so bad as to disqualify him from his university post after the war. His crimes had been specially obnoxious since he happened to be the author of a standard book on Old Testament ethics. He had truly practised what he had not preached. He was now at the Conference of Old Testament Studies and atoned symbolically for his misdeeds by offering his scholarly services to the Jewish members. At this conference, too, for the first time the presence of scholars from Israel accentuated the newness of biblical studies.

Israel! Unforeseen its holocaust, unforeseen its rise from the ashes! Even more unforeseen the consequences of the making of the tiny state on the shores of the eastern Mediterranean! What is Israel? Who is a Jew? Is Israel the utopia of an oppressed minority or the overweening ambition of Herzl and his followers? Does Zionism pave the way to the age of the Messiah and spell out the fulfilment of prophecy? Is the Return to the Homeland a religious event, God calling his people home? Or are the Qibbutzim from the start a negation of God and a socialist enterprise, secular through and through? Are the Jews the victims of a conspiracy which has lured them to certain destruction in the furnace of Palestine, or are they tools of imperialist western money to dispossess the rightful inhabitants of that land? There is not a label of praise, nor an indictment of crime, which cannot be attached to the making of Israel. Israel the capitalist pawn, the imperialist disease, the foreign intruder on the one hand, David victorious over Goliath, the instrument of God's providence, the centre of the meaning of history on the other!

Christian triumphalism had nothing to do with the making of Israel. As I sat at the radio with my cousin's husband Uriel, who was to shine later in the diplomatic service before he became a professor at the Hebrew University, I became aware of another world. Again it was one of fear and trembling. The massacres of millions in India, following independence, had not troubled us much. But Palestine was a different matter and the ending of the British Mandate in 1948 was preceded by violence and reprisals. It left a bitter taste on all sides. At the United Nations the British, more than aware of the future dangers, suffered by a stroke of irony defeat at the hands of the U.S.A. and the U.S.S.R. My friend Uriel followed every word of the debate which led to Britain being outmanoeuvred and outvoted. Not only the Americans, but also the Russians, said Yes to the birth of Israel.

The war between Jews and Arabs followed, the first of many to come. Uriel had no doubt about survival and success. Israel was there to stay, to take root, to yield fruit, to welcome home the dispersed, and to breed a new generation of free boys and girls. Uriel was strong and not mystical. For him this Passover was secular and political, and as the years passed and the reality took shape his generation eschewed the utopian strain of Messianism.

Both Jews and Christians longed to see Israel develop

normally. My friends, like Uriel, wished to suppress the religious question mark. One heard of orthodox Jews resisting secular Zionism; they not only stoned buses on the sabbath but treated all but themselves as apostates from the narrow Messianic ideal. You could hardly meet a Jew anywhere who interpreted the foundation of the state of Israel in the same manner, but the interpretation did not matter. The task in hand sufficed and the Israel-born Sabra had to work and fight hard. Identity was achieved in a remarkable way, considering that the exiles came from all kinds of backgrounds, classes, and cultures. A romantic tinge attended the flight of the Yemenite Jews to the homeland, to the groundswell of Arab hatred. The dragons' teeth were truly sown.

I could not be content with such spiritual indifference. Israel could not be divorced from the past, from the exaltation and humiliation of thirty centuries. Some of her teachers were alive to the challenge of the holocaust and asked if the face of God could be the same after the catastrophe. If it was not, what was the 'new' face, if any? I also deviated from the thoughts of heaven in order to interpret Auschwitz, if possible by relating the crucified with the gassed, in both suffering and in resurrection. Needless to say, Uriel and his circles were deaf to such an enterprise.

But the state of Israel became an equally haunting obsession of the mind. To me it seemed natural to link the new with the old. This could be done in a variety of ways. The biblical story begins with Abraham and the patriarchal movements in tents. Jacob, who becomes Israel, is the typical representative of the nation, for he fights and submits in the battle for life. He is wholly practical, concerned with flocks, food, shelter, clothes, and places; but he is also mystical, a dreamer of God and angels, a fighter with the demonic unknown, lamed in the spiritual struggle for the knowledge of God. He is one who knows God and who is known of God. The whole narrative of the nation retains this ambiguity. It never fails to retain the tension between the temporal and the eternal. The sons of Jacob still reflect the divine presence and the secular terror as they betray their brother and are at last reconciled to Joseph in Egypt. As the Epistle to the Hebrews insists, this tale of men is also the story of God, of witnesses to the Presence in the absence. Moses, Joshua, Gideon, Samson, the prophets give continuity to the fragmentation of history. How, then, could Israel now be without the eternal meaning which redeems history, whether in acclamation or in lamentation, in laughter or with tears? How could one not pray for the peace of Jerusalem, and thus savour the eternal city and the temporal upheaval in the light of the truth? Israel, as I saw it, established a fulcrum, a centre, a nucleus, which attracted all the nations' displeasure, aggression, and threats to the future of mankind. Normality was the last thing to be hoped for in the creation of this state.

But my Christian friends, if at all interested, did not want to share this view either. The trend in the fifties was not eschatological but humanistic. The proliferation of world-wide conferences furthered the cause of church unity. The Church of South India seemed to steer the course of ecumenical progress. American money poured into new institutions. The Christian religion was to be 'enjoyed' and 'used' in the building up of peace and prosperity. Anglicans reaffirmed 'Firm Faith' in terms of stability, and a Board of Social Responsibility and Education investigated problems connected with the family. Birth control, artificial insemination, abortion, and divorce were subjects to be tackled. The demands of the new age had to be reconciled with principles of tradition. The spirit of reform touched on everything, whether matters of liturgy or education. The sociological diapason seemed to swallow the original tune. Poor Jacob! Bethel and the ford of Jabbok could hardly count in the greatest transformation of human history. Jet aircraft, sputniks, and microbiology hardly authenticated an eschatological feeling for events. Christians were not only glad of the respite granted after the threat of nuclear destruction. They wanted it to go on for ever.

This refusal to confront the hostile world crept, like a virus, into the Christian body. We moved in a world of plenty, of gadgets, holidays, insurance, success. The tower of Babel was rebuilt and looked fine. I shared the blindness and deafness of my peers, but one day, arriving early at the College, I faced the incoming transport of little animals. The lift to the laboratories was stacked high with rabbits, mice, rats, and guinea-pigs. On inquiry I learnt that this restocking of the laboratories was a daily affair, and I concluded that it must be going on all over the world. Our ecological rape and torture spread its invisible power to every corner of the globe. The Hideous Strength, which C.S. Lewis had written about, encountered no resistance. I denounced and lamented at all seasons, a voice first in the wilderness, then in communion with the eccentric few. But the Christians, like Esau, sold their birthright, to eat the porridge of progressive medicine and a false humanism. Shaw, of all people, was right when in *St Joan* he articulated the truth: 'You don't know; you haven't seen. . .you madden yourself with words. . .but when you see the thing. . .'[1] The changes which came over the world were not seen and when they became tangible and irrefutable they were accepted. The world could say that it had overcome the Spirit.

---

[1] Scene vi and Epilogue. The Chaplain de Stogumber's 'shock' comes from *seeing* the death.

13

THE MAKING OF A VOLCANO

By the middle fifties I was a typical householder outside London. A modest property with a tolerable mortgage housed a growing family. I taught, researched, wrote, preached, and officiated occasionally. I enjoyed the growing stimulation of London's music and theatres and discovered the joys of gardening. I returned as a visitor to Europe, climbed in the Alps, swam in the ocean off Cornwall and Scotland. I joined in the joys of the flesh and adhered to the gospel of security and progressive betterment for all. We know very little of the undercurrents, and our *hubris* leads to our nemesis in ignorance and even innocence. We forget our demonic nature. We obey our Faustian urge, always striving and never content, but we dream of ourselves in a paradise of peace, where we bathe in the sun. We would be great, yet without becoming murderers like Macbeth. We desire friends, yet without becoming disillusioned like Timon of Athens. We surround ourselves with comforts as if we were to stay on this earth for ever, in wilful defiance of the whole tragic tradition. We built up the old wastes during the fifties. A new generation was born, nurtured on the best that food and care could provide. The children were immunized against disease and the good life was offered to the eye (photography), the ear (Hi-Fi equipment), the palate (wines and spirits), the senses (perfumes and deodorants), and sexual activity.

But this gratification of pleasures only obscured the measure of the political, economic, and scientific forces at work. Entertainment and sport flourished as never before. They bit deeply into our culture. Men and women, glued to the new wonder of television, little knew that they were being changed. As they exposed themselves to the sights and sounds an old world passed away. The fissions, however, were barely recognizable in the daily routine, for they were deep down, below in the heart of mankind. The volcano was

112

in the making, and we did not know it yet. I sensed the build-
up of these vast energies not through a ghastly apocalypse,
but through a private introduction to a project in the College.
An electronic brain was being built, the forerunner of many
millions of computers and the programming of human lots.

The volcanic forces are most dangerous when the earth
keeps quiet. As all the inhabitants of San Francisco Bay
know, the fault which runs through the earth needs regular
relief, and little quakes are welcome. In the fifties nothing
shook or quaked. Workers' revolts in Berlin, Hungary, and
Poland were scotched easily with mechanized forces of the
Red Army. The lava flowed miserably from these isolated
eruptions. The saliva of propaganda drowned the cries of
despair and the appeals for help. I listened to the East German
radio and had my fill of lies, announced in the tone which
the Communists had gladly inherited in direct succession
from Goebbels.

The scientific advance took the place of religion in the
Eastern block and went hand in hand with military planning
and social engineering, including slave labour. The Russians
had always excelled in the probing of the spheres, and now
the Chinese, too, joined their traditional expertise in the
investigation of constellations and galaxies. Their successes
were no longer meant to yield a spiritual harvest, for the
working masses live in a cosmos from which all non-
materialistic meaning must be excluded. They, like us,
became materialists *in toto*. For the first time in human
history did cosmic research free itself from a meaningful
cosmology. Atoms and molecules moved, attracted, repelled,
radiated in a cosmos which could also be called chaos if
names meant anything. Did names mean anything, or did
language convey any function? Philosophers turned to this
question as their main task and disdained to ask and answer
comprehensive theories of the universe. Metaphysics beat
its great retreat into linguistics. This abdication also percolated
through to the people. We are what we are, and the world is
what it is.

Such a positivism is logical, pervasive, and immoral. Even
in England, most conservative of countries, the old system
creaked. It could not hold out against the hedonistic erosion

from within nor the scientific persuasions from without. But the volcano was not yet ready to erupt. The ship lurched towards secularism without foundering. Its prophets Shaw and Wells now received foreign reinforcement. Voices which had flourished abroad for decades at last reached these shores. I marvelled to greet old friends and enemies in their translated guise at last. Freud, who had died in England in 1939, now justified millions in a new attitude to sex and guilt. His jargon — inferiority complex, Oedipus complex, overcompensation, etc. — passed from mouth to mouth. Jung ran a poor second, though his 'archetypes' also figured in conversation and were to affect the religious scene. But far more important, because socially penetrating, was the neo-Marxist crusade, which popularized the unreadable *Das Kapital* in paperbacks. The antique Left Book Club of Gollancz was now overtaken by a ruder tone, and when Brecht appeared in the theatre and in print I realized that we had come a long way.

Brecht had been one of the major figures of the theatre in Berlin before Hitler. Of working-class and provincial origin he had inherited, and reacted against, the great German tradition. Though dramatic in feeling and expression he did not wish to perpetuate the tragic and comic effect of the stage. He wanted to use the stage to undermine bourgeois culture, even though he wrote for the bourgeoisie. Similarly his poems were thoroughly lyrical, but the intention was not to foster the moral climate of goodness, beauty, and truth. Brecht was the genius of a bitter revolution who took the old tag 'Der Mensch ist was er isst'[1] to stamp our present and future with the materialism of the left. Though not a comfortable party-man and at the end running foul of the Communist bosses in Berlin, he did more than anyone to tear the last vestiges of Christian belief from our hearts. A host of lesser writers and producers learnt from him, and left-wing theatre had become in Berlin the most powerful institution against Hitler. No wonder the storm-troopers attacked these *Left Columns* with arms and explosives.

---

[1] 'Man is what he eats'.

Brecht's *The Threepenny Opera*[1] had been a huge success in Berlin in 1928. The London riff-raff of murderers, cutthroats, frauds, smugglers, prostitutes worked wonders on the stage. It was good entertainment, if only because Kurt Weill's tunes were memorable. They could be hummed immediately afterwards as any good 'hit'. But the words had the real bite. They clawed at propriety, morality, nice manners, decency, and fine sentiments. Take away the layer of cosy self-deceit, said Brecht, and behold with cold eyes and hearts: there is the thing, mankind, voraciously prying and pouncing. Brecht elevated brutality in order to force upon us a socialism, bereft of utopian enthusiasm or even the pretence of the twaddle of freedom. When I first heard the opera I was in the presence of a new disclosure, a world fascinating and powerful. Brecht released one from the myth of spiritual power and moral categories. He mediated Marxist–Leninism with the cheekiness of the spluttering saxophone. In exile he did not change this tune, though he went to the U.S.A. and not to the U.S.S.R. (he valued survival after all!). Chicago's stockyards supplied material for satire and the course of the war until 1945 evoked a series of polemical successes.

Brecht's plays reached London only after the long lapse of time, but now *Mother Courage* and the *Caucasian Chalk Circle* and many other plays answered to, and stimulated, an aggressively anti-religious, materialistic, revolutionary trend. England seemed to me to capitulate to foreign forces and ideas, and I even flattered myself and the English that they were the victims of a conspiracy. This was not so. A new spirit was abroad, a volcanic element in protest against suburban bourgeois standards. It required no open anti-religious platform, nor did it make do with non-conformist attitudes. The old age of ethical atheism, too, had set. Brecht pioneered a whole host of entirely English plays, mostly for television, in which king and country, god and religion, were mocked as the ridiculous but nevertheless dangerous properties of a vanishing reactionary class. One example is a

---

[1] *Die Dreigroschenoper* was based upon John Gay's *The Beggar's Opera*, first performed in 1728 and successfully revived in 1920.

series which went on for years, appropriately entitled 'Till Death us do part', sacred words taken from the marriage service in the Book of Common Prayer. To my amazement Christians, clergy and laity alike, loved this show and laughed. I wondered if this could be the same talent of humour which had defeated Nazi propaganda. I soon found that this was not so. The Brechtian–Marxist onslaught in its new brutal colours came from within.

I could entertain no illusions about the intention of the new school for it wanted power. It derided the tradition not as a *jeu d'esprit*, but, in league with trade-union leaders and the budding student left, it worked towards the destruction of the establishment. It scorned law, order, freedom, and worship. For me, by now immersed in Dante, Brecht and his disciples were 'devil's disciples', for they were bent upon bringing down heaven and the cosmic unity in love, and to raise hell in suspicion and hatred. The degradation of the divine and the mutilation of the spirit were the prelude to the grand take-over. Milton's Pandemonium, shorn of all beauty and reduced to working-class meanness in speech and manners, was to serve. The collective was being formed in the underground.

Christians, as we have seen, are pacific and make bold claims for non-resistance to evil. Yet I was surprised and angered by the total silence with which the church leaders reacted to militant atheism. Some did not seem to know and were too busy with administration; others were too stupid to register the pressures beneath; a significant, though small, section already joined the new forces, ready to fill high places in the secular religion of the future.

I looked around for mentors and comforters. There were none. Bell had died in 1958, aged 75. Many of my colleagues were unaware of the great betrayal in the wings and sympathized with what they called 'progress', since 'there must be change'. Professionals hide under their professionalism, as Kierkegaard and Unamuno knew many years before. The favourite game was also taken over from Germany and it called itself *Entmythologisierung*. This terrible word could never be rendered in English, but its message came across with simplicity. Take the 'myth' out of the Christian faith

116

and you are left with a workable nucleus which the modern man can operate. This was not really new, for the nineteenth century had already baulked at mythology. George Eliot, translator of Strauss's *Life of Jesus*, had seriously parodied the 'key to all mythologies' in her novel *Middlemarch*. But memories are short, and she was forgotten for a while and Rudolf Bultmann of Marburg became the prophet of the unmythical Allah.

This Professor of the New Testament had endeavoured to preach the gospel in Nazi Germany to a generation bred in scientific knowledge. He had absorbed a certain amount of language from Heidegger. His insistence on the here and now made him attractive to English ears in the fifties, who had abandoned the there and then, heaven and hell, miracles and resurrection and ascension. Bultmann was a historian who had to find Christ outside this mythical history of virgin birth and the conquest over rulers and demonic powers. Yet when I checked his credentials I was not impressed, for, though not a Nazi, he seemed to me to have failed even as a preacher of the Word. His sermon on 22 June 1941 — the day when the German armies invaded Russia — interpreted the story of the great banquet from Luke ch. 14, the traditional Gospel for that Sunday. Bultmann drew then the inevitable parallel: Christian people do not come to the wedding; money, power, pleasures, technical progress, sport are preferred, and the state threatens. We have failed, we have not served the community in need. We cannot recognize the disguised God until we free ourselves from this world, to view our life as provisional, trustful in the dark and without fantasies. Inner detachment and Christian vigilance answer to the terrifying crisis. All this is very well, I thought, though it comes under the Brechtian axe. Is not this well-meant moralizing taking the place of a straightforward denunciation, stopping short of direct action or indirect conspiracy, cushioning the 'we' with their own troubles in the syrup of self-pity?

I could never see the point of this type of reductionism. If the Comedy is no longer Divine and the golden bowl smashed — so be it! Words will not alter the facts. Throw out poetry and symbolical richness, the ancient frieze of priests

117

coming to the sacrifice, of beautiful boys and maidens, of warriors in their chariots, and the seamless robe of the universe is torn to shreds. With heaven and hell out of the way what could stop the eruption of the volcano of secularism? If you talk of God, you talk of yourself: self-understanding is all you can hope for. Jesus is unknowable, his preaching irrecoverable, and 'the empty tomb' only an obstacle to faith. Bultmann's new friends talked endlessly of 'authentic existence' and 'freedom for the future', which you were supposed to encounter in the proclamation of the Word. But this Word no longer allowed you to see the heavens opened and the glory of God in its myriad reflections in the creation. I came to loathe this religion stripped of cosmic dimensions and objective tokens of the divine presence. In England it developed a particularly hateful character of arrogant superiority. It sided with left-wing politics, of which it never took the proper Marxist measure, and pushed the churches into the role of an unattractive agency for 'doing good', i.e. persuading and blackmailing other perople to back up secular causes. Christian secularism undermined the fabric of faith with pretensions of 'knowing better' or 'best'.

English apostasy was exposed by a mean little book called *Honest to God*. The author, John Robinson, acted as a kind of catalyst for the religious dishonesty towards God which Bultmann's demythologization had begun. The book, published in 1963, came at the end of an epoch of decline. It was a success in copies sold, though I hardly ever met anyone who read it right through. Robinson scored by crowning the pervading emptiness with total confusion. He mixed and misinterpreted others to buttress his thesis that God is not 'out there' and that human conduct obeys no objective divine laws. In England ethics and religion had always stood in a harmonious and fertile relationship, inasmuch as God is the highest good. But now if God could be left out of human behaviour the good also became a questionable substance, if only in view of the endless diversities in human behaviour. How could anyone maintain a standard of right when a survey in one part of the world showed that evil there could be tolerated here, and vice versa? Ethical norms (say on matters such as infanticide, polygamy, promiscuity, homosexuality) were relative, as the humanists had always maintained. All this had been known before, but now the self-appointed religious leaders were in the frontline of backing up permissiveness. The devils' slogan 'All is permitted' re-entered the arena of stupified spectators as if it were new. I witnessed the breaking-up of marriages, of mothers abandoning their families, of children attacking and milking their parents. The world of Sodom and Gomorrah exploded in little suburban homes, and the sanction for the miserable deviations from duty was found in the ever-available word 'Love'. Love became the trump-card for doing the next best thing in 'situations'. Love also became the sanctimonious title-deed for evading obligations and escaping censure. In the name of Love it was assumed that you did not have to pay for the consequences of evil deeds, which were no longer to be called 'evil'. Retributive justice was foiled when the guilty were seen to be victims of their circumstances only. We were all disturbed, and it was only a question of degree whether our disturbances showed. No ethics could be further removed from the prophetic bedrock conviction that 'Man is shown what is right', that man can and must 'do justice, love mercy, and walk humbly with God'. The prophets' wail of incurable wounds, their call of a trial to establish the truth, their prayer for healing, and their promise of gracious renewal, was now swamped in a sloppy permissive 'honesty', presided over by a nebulous Jesus.

I reacted to this new flood with cynical laughter. It amused me to think that this stuff could be thought original. Dostoyevsky had faced the amoralists over a century ago and had demonstrated the inner connection between the liberal 'all is permitted' and the murderous consequences. Nietzsche had advocated the 'new' morality, and superman had travelled from him through Shaw into the English language. Gide had popularized himself as the immoralist. Somehow this previous generation had endowed their polemics with wit and style. The new theological twist lacked all subtlety. I realized that its boredom would frustrate its teaching and that the nine-days' wonder could not last. But I also noted the potency of the poison in the churches and among individual Christians. They had no defences, except their majestic liturgies and rituals. Here, at least, seemed to be an unassailable refuge of the eternal in time. But I underestimated the determination of the radical theologians for they also located the strength of Christian conviction in the citadel of worship, and hence trained their guns on the sanctuary and priesthood. If they could secularize the Eucharist they would have chased their honest God out of the mystery of life.

Cynicism is a weapon of doubtful quality. Even in secular combat it ruins the character of the fighter. Most of our administrators in the collective show the grey shadow of cynicism around their lustreless eyes. But in spiritual combat cynicism cannot win because it has no hope and no love. I felt emptied by my own cynicism in trying to come to terms with the cold villainy in theological circles. But how was one to react to their treachery? I could not simply side with conservative fundamentalism, a biblical literalism, which now also entered the stage in the shape of crusades, led by Billy Graham. These mass meetings meant nothing to me. I had, after all, shared the ecstasy of pre-Nazi Communist meetings in the Berlin Sportpalast, and the Christ fanaticism, spurred on by chanting hymns and repeating slogans, seemed very tame in comparison.

The curious thing about religious developments in the fifties was the amalgam of naivety, feeding on ignorance, and crafty wire-pulling by the arrogant and self-styled progressives. The 'most smiling, smooth, detested parasites, courteous destroyers, affable wolves, meek bears'[1] advanced in church and state as England seemed to ape the German miracle of economic recovery.

[1] *Timon of Athens*, III. 6, 105-6.

14

DEATH OF THE DEAD GOD

The impact of the new theology could be felt everywhere. On the one hand, the media opened their doors to the new trend, which culminated in the cult of the 'dead God'. Ironically the phrase that God had died or is dead was quite stale, but so great was the ignorance or malice of the profiteers in the new religion that they pretended the phrase to be new, as if coined by themselves. Protests to the effect that, among others, Nietzsche had himself used the phrase in his *Thus spake Zarathustra* and *Antichrist*, by quoting it from the French atheists and Jean Paul and Schopenhauer, did nothing to undermine the popular confidence in the 'God is dead' or new theology. Similarly systematic counter-attacks, as by Mascall in *The Secularization of Christianity*, failed despite theological and stylistic excellence of wit. The West wanted to bury its ancient god, and nothing could deter its secular arm from digging the grave.

This death-wish may be compared to the elm-disease which struck the country a little later. The virus was carried by a beetle which flies in the air, and nothing could be done to stop its devastation. Similarly, churches and colleges were struck by the infection, and the old medicines, namely of prayer and asceticism, proved not so much ineffective as unavailable. Men ceased to pray and to fast, and the devils could not be tamed.

This rebellion against the spiritual tradition had, as we have shown, been in preparation for several decades. It was the climax of upheavals such as the civilized world had not experienced before. Yet it came from within and had the full assent of people hitherto called religious or good. If ever there has been a free decision in the area of spiritual willing and doing, this reformation must rank as the most daunting example.

It was triggered off by the social conscience in England.

The Marxist Left were right, it was felt, in their criticism of religion. For too long nothing had been changed. Christianity, the most revolutionary movement in its origins, had become a conservative force. It favoured property and continuity of class privileges. The result was that Christians were not at all 'doing good', except in a condescending sort of way. But the age of paternalism was over, and should have been over sooner if only Christians had not tampered with the evils of the time. Now was the time of real change: to look after the destitute, to house the homeless, and to bring relief to the underdeveloped and underprivileged masses overseas. True Christianity dealt with the naked and the hungry, and since God was too dead to help them, it was left to organizations, such as Oxfam, to do the job for him.

This appeal to the good nature of Christians revived the ancient strand of social activism and was amazingly successful. It soon enveloped even the liturgical life of the churches. They had already taken in hand certain reforms. They modernized their language and transformed the centre of gravity in liturgy from the praise of the infinite God to that of caring for men. Although prayer to God ceased to be meaningful the reformers gave ample scope to very long perorations to the dead God for all sorts and conditions of men. The old Prayer Book, as all liturgies, had never ignored these – rulers, ruled, those at risk, the sick, the dead, the bereaved; but now this terse series was replaced by spontaneous *ad hoc* utterances, interspersed with pauses, in which whole continents, countries, regions, districts, streets were named, and practically the whole of the news, domestic and foreign, was placed before the Almighty. Since this Almighty never deigned to act or react, it followed that these petitions and intercessions could be no more than collective self-projections, the articulations of soliloquizing groups, which hoped to boost their own morale by talk. The conseqence of this practice could be felt in the increasing democratization of public worship and the erosion of the hierarchical structure. When everyone could be 'priest after the order of Melchizedek', and priestesses were to be included in this order, the old order must cease.

This democratization met with hardly any opposition. Some, it is true, simply left the Church and ceased to attend services. Their number was not insignificant. The loyalists, however, stuck it out and underwrote banalities and even vulgarities which they would not have tolerated before the breaking-up of society. Here was a cultural decline indeed, and its symptoms were linguistic. God was soon addressed as 'you', and his presence was desired to preserve mankind from the trial. The suburban longing for security had prevailed, and a spiritual mediocrity now had to serve instead of a Christian working through life as the ordeal which it is.

As these pages have shown *ad nauseam*, the interpretation of our history must bring out its irony. The turn of events soon made nonsense of the new religion. It was still paternalistic, *de haut en bas*, and only ceased to be so when the resources of the bourgeoisie grew scanty and there remained little slack for the luxury of giving. Paternalism vanished with a succession of financial crises. Soon those who had indulged in giving a helping hand would need it themselves, and they had never thought along those lines. The people had been grossly misled in the belief that a non-transcendental, boring, worthy, improving, and thoroughly non-tragic and inglorious substitute could replace the old religion.

How had the confidence trick been played and why had it succeeded? Partly it resulted from the infiltration of careerists into the Christian fold. The modern wolves who came in sheeps' clothing had an uncanny hold on the lambs. The tale of the false shepherds had come full circle. They had replaced the Lord, the shepherd of the Bible, with their own pipings. To my infinite horror and disgust they used the name of Dietrich Bonhoeffer to make good their assault, for this name had by now acquired a modern sanctity which authorized secularism — a religion without God.

It was a stroke of crowning cruelty, an insult to the memory of a martyr. Never before had a martyr's death been invoked against his own testimony as in the case of Dietrich Bonhoeffer. The background explains much. After a long silence — his name had not been made famous in England until about 1955 — the *Letters from Prison* had made their impact. These and his other writings came to England via translations made in the U.S.A. Thus much of the directness was lost, and, worse still, the *Letters* were read partly as one reads an ordinary correspondence, partly as a kind of devotional manual. The *Letters* became the source of utter confusion.

Misled by radical exploiters Bonhoeffer was made the spokesman of ideas totally alien to him. Clichés were taken out of the context of the letters and soon the religious world was bombarded with the secular gospel, in which the sacred and the secular were one, and the world had come of age, where we had come to a maturity which could get along without God, living 'as if he did not exist'. Religionless Christianity became a popular tag taken from the Bonhoeffer stable. It did not occur to people to question the legitimacy of these quotations and to wonder why a man, engaged to be married, should risk his neck and die for Christ.

Bonhoeffer was used as the exponent of an impatience with religion itself, with the whole business of God as enacted in the past. Severed from the environment in which he wrote and suffered he seemed to give his authority to abandon revelation, miracle, prayer, and divinity. Jesus, the man for others, could really be any man, and soon Bonhoeffer's work was reduced to 'man-for-others' ciphers, interpreted as one thought fit. The obvious argument against such a doctrine of God and Christ, namely that it did not require the elaborate structure of the Bible and tradition to make this banal appeal, and that it was not likely to work at any time, was dismissed with a superior arrogance, which to me at least belied the motivation behind the Bonhoeffer cult.

This false cult should have ended conclusively with the publication of Bethge's monumental biography of Bonhoeffer in 1967. Bethge also lectured in America and in England to put the record straight. He showed with irrefutable clarity that his friend had always been a man of God in the biblical sense, that he had grown and changed, struggled for Christian existence, and that the *Letters* were, as one should have expected, a chance collection. That they were smuggled out of prison, and that they survived at all, is to be remembered as much as the fact that not everything could be said, and that what was said belonged to a definite period in history. Letters are not dogma.

Bonhoeffer's work, though incomplete and sadly cut

short, can now be seen as a part of the proper undertaking to combine biblical foundations with modern, existential, rational critiques of the Christian life. The Person of Christ, the ethics of the Christian, the communion of the faithful, speak and are spoken to within the chaos of the twentieth century. The focus is, no doubt, the Man, as in all Christian theology. Bonhoeffer spans the world of the highest humanity (Berlin-Grunewald, as I knew it, with its music, warmth, rigorous learning, tradition) and the lowest mob. His memorial stands in his Act and Being, the convergence of God and man in our midst.

Bethge's reclaiming of the truth took some time to reach the reading public, but at length the humbug surrounding the dead God died like any fashion. Nevertheless, it left a nasty taste in the world of religion, which never quite recovered the rigours of the theological quest for truth. The *Letters*, how-ever, have achieved their proper status as a classic of con-temporary spirituality, and Bethge's biography remains one of the primary pillars of the spiritual interpretation of our times. It raises anew the question how we can be against the world to which we belong, seek for community in frag-mented human society, and believe in God whom we repudiate. Far from short-circuiting these age-old problems in an insipid religionless Christianity or a system of minimal moral behaviour, Bonhoeffer proves that these problems pertain to our condition as children of God.

15

PREDICAMENT AND RENEWAL

Throughout the post-war development I had rightly felt that God, the eternal, could not be put through the mill of our ephemeral concerns. Religious relevance could only kill God, if he could be killed. It would adapt him to every whim and the big Chief would resemble all the miserable little chiefs around us. Passing fancies would feed the image of a Christ who was only a mirror of what we were ourselves. Clearly, a non-transcendent and changeable Deity could be anything but God, and attempts to replace him with morality had already failed.

I erred, however, in underestimating the pressures of our scientific and mechanized world. When Hitler was defeated I had thought that we could all breathe again. I never doubted that our cultural heritage was strong enough to attain new dimensions of popularity and that millions would enjoy what had been denied them before. To a certain extent this hope was fulfilled, especially in England where the radio (BBC 3), some television, and cheap books handed on the classical heritage to a new generation. The post-war world received an amazing impetus from the past. This accessibility of greatness was not only a technical wonder but also a spiritual joy, unprecedented in the annals of civilization.

Nevertheless, I erred in my religious evaluation of these riches. I had imagined that, to take an example, the availability of Dante's *Divine Comedy* would draw the new readers into the centre of Christian belief, just as I still fondly conceived of Shakespeare's works as a bulwark for freedom. But I did not know that the greatness of human art may inspire men quite apart from their content. Thus it is conceivable that you can listen to Haydn's great final masses (and they were virtually unknown before the post-war renaissance) or even perform in Monteverdi's 'Magnificat' without subscribing to the *Credo* implicit in the texts. I had, of course, known this secularization of the sacred in the days of my boyhood when we attended the Bach 'Passion' under Bruno Walter, and hardly anyone in the auditorium gave their spiritual assent to the Gospel. But this had been a special case. Now the cultural excellence replaced the religious cultus in a broader sweep. Only the Communists still desisted from playing 'sacred' music since, at least in Russia, the commissariat detects a danger in conveying words which may conceivably be taken to be meaningful and true.

The Catholic leadership, however, had to face modern secularity with unexpected results. Immediately after the death of Pius XII the world arrived in full force at the doors of St Peter's. In the past the Church had overcome its foes by resistance and compromise. Nationalism had been absorbed and even modernism accommodated. The scientific revolution had never shaken the foundations of dogma. But now more was at stake than a set of discoveries or a political movement, although all these added to the loss of nerve. The lid had been firmly fixed on the volcano, and now the suppressed energies united to force an eruption. The Catholic Church had to come to terms with the same energies which I had underestimated in our own context. John XXIII, aged 77, cast a brilliant and benign shadow over the preparations for, and the proceedings of, the famous *aggiornamento*. John was the son of the people and the father of the people. Christians everywhere welcomed his warmth. The peasant from Bergamo was nearer our heart than the exclusive aristocrat who had departed. One could not help responding to the Pope who embraced and kissed an Archbishop of Canterbury and an Eastern Patriarch, and who advanced to greet a Rabbi, saying: 'I am Joseph, your brother'.

John seemed to give the lie to our cynical judgement that individual personality no longer mattered. Pius XII had not been without charisma, but this new Pope had the peculiar charisma suitable to the age. He was distinguished, yet poor; open-hearted, yet disciplined; intelligent but not remotely intellectual. He was serious, but also fun. He seemed to spell an end to the sickly sweet pictures of saintliness which distorted so many Catholic churches. No wonder one could trust such a man, who personified the tradition, not by announcing 'Io sono la tradizione' (attributed to Pius IX before 1870), but by humbly living the gospel. He broke with the subtle ways of diplomacy and secrecy and when he 'packed his bags' before he died in 1963, he had not only the Catholic world at his feet but even his enemies. Pope John who received Khrushchev in Rome seemed to symbolize the victory of a man over the stranglehold of institutions.

During the brief years of his pontificate John underlined both the attractiveness of charismatic personality and its tragic bounds. There could be no return to Jesus, as if the intervening centuries had never occurred. The man was no longer enough: *ecce homo* could not be the answer to vast problems of high complexity. Even under John the Church mattered more than Jesus, for the Church mediates his presence. I could not help wondering if John, perhaps against his will, erected just another façade.

Yet I greeted John's unique work before and during the second Vatican Council with enthusiasm. No one else could have held together the polarized parties in his church. Ever since the modernist controversy the ghosts of Loisy and Tyrrell had brooded over the western European branches of Catholicism, calling for freedom of expression, the abolition of secrecy and censorship. The tension between authoritarianism and democratization had threatened a break, for how could lovers of liberty bend under the rigid demands of a remote centre? Before Vatican II authors had to get their books past the censor and were driven to the subterfuge of inserting acceptable clichés to make sure of success. Moral and legal problems were sent to Rome for an answer and interminable delays, not to mention expense, wearied the suppliants. The whole apparatus was in the reactionary hands who had sided with Hitler and Mussolini during the Spanish Civil War. Their outlook was as monolithic as that of all dictatorships. They could point to their massive institutions all over the world as evidence for the rightness of an authoritarian regime. Hospitals and colleges flourished and spread, not because of freedom of thought, but through obedience in sacrifice.

The problem of authority, therefore, governs all other aspects of Catholic life, and it could not be solved simply by the beautiful *Tu es Petrus* of the liturgical chant. Even John, the saintly man, could not of himself state and dictate what was right or wrong in human society. Practical decisions and theoretical considerations are always at loggerheads, as soon as ethical problems come to the fore. Whether we deal with capital and property, the rights and duties of the individual, the family and sexual laws and prohibitions, the aims and methods of education, medical care, etc., we cannot expect the *Papa* to rule as Jesus may have done among the Twelve. The delegation of authority, however, always relied on primary principles, and these principles went back to the Lord himself.

Before Vatican II rumblings had been heard inside the volcano, but they had been suppressed, though not entirely so. Many of my Catholic friends indicated that the *Una Sancta* was neither unified nor holy, but engaged in unholy controversy. But they also enjoyed the fight and hardly bothered to disguise their delight in ending the long period of secrecy. Jesuits and Dominicans, once the guardians of militant controls, openly sided with the new freedom. Some of their demands went very far, for they shook the foundations of Catholic tradition. They scorned the priestly privilege and the hierarchical structure and already whispered about a married priesthood.

We had certainly come a long way from the days when I was refused entry into the monastery because I wore a fringe which made me look like a girl. Then Mass had been celebrated in Latin only. Now concessions to the language spoken by the people had quite transformed the rite. First the gospel, later the epistle, and soon parts of the canon would be heard in the vernacular. I was startled to hear all sorts of dialects in Africa during the liturgy. In America, too, the young ordinands had little use for Latin, since they acquired only a trivial amount for a mechanical recital. But their linguistic poverty was only part of the story. They looked to liturgy not as a supernatural drama, but as the means of finding God in one another. Latin was certainly a barrier and only their own language could effectively communicate in the search for divine fellowship. The high ritual which culminates in the change of the elements alienated these advocates of a humane open community. Before Vatican II they still read about transubstantiation to pass their examinations, but they hardly believed in it, if it meant anything to them at all. After Vatican II they dismissed the doctrine as dangerous, a survival of magic. With their missals now cut down to simple texts, in their spoken language, they confronted their former teachers as victors.

The older generation of bishops and priests suffered from this aggression and even spoke of treachery. They suspected the ecumenical mingling. Having come from humble homes and having worked to get to the top, they were affronted by the largely pampered offspring of Catholic parents who had prospered. This warfare between the old and the new came into an unforgettable service of ordination near San Francisco which I attended. The chapel still spoke of the *ancien régime*, baroque and authoritarian, and the bishop with his entourage proceeded as if the old forms still prevailed. Silence and reverence attended the introit, but soon the huge congregation were seized by the opposing spirit of youth, and during the elevation there were spontaneous scenes of rejoicing. The bishop stood like a marble statue at the altar to administer the sacrament, but the young sang, laughed, wept, danced in the nave. Even the lovely girls joined in, and the bishop still stood, as if frozen, on the steps. Eventually the young received communion, holding hands, slightly swaying. After the liturgy they confessed that they had been 'turned on', and the elders bemoaned the passing of a faith. The humble and poor of the past, who had become corporately rich, saw the disintegration of the body. We saw the end of an epoch in which the Church had served immigrant paupers, and the beginning of another in which alienated youth, born and bred in a rich land, sought a role.

Before Vatican II such occurrences would have been impossible. But the reforming spirits, with John at their head, did not know that they were handling hot lava, bursting out of the social and spiritual volcanoes in many parts of the world. I also shared this ignorance, for my theological studies had acquainted me with the highly respectable liberal wing of French and German Catholicism, and élite of culture and breeding, a kind of buffer-state between the extremists of the right and of the left. It no more occurred to me, than to them, that they would ultimately be squeezed out of their reforming roles by revolutionary upstarts. People like Daniélou, de Vaux, de Lubac, Congar in France, and Rahner in Innsbruck, and Urs von Balthasar in Einsiedeln and Basel, were quite outstanding in learning. For them the Bible and the tradition were inseparable, and they could guide the Church from a defunct black clericalism to the genuine body of creative freedom and inspiring, enjoyable, self-authenticating truth. They were not only amenable to, but actively engaged in, reforms, which would remove the signs of sterility and old prejudices. Faded flowers, rosaries said *ad infinitum*, ugly statues, censorship, and ethnic hangovers, as still found in Antisemitism or in Catholic minority ghettoes, could and must yield to a renewed Catholicism of the highest standards, in which grace and knowledge were at one.

The strength of these renewing voices lay in their unique authority. Trained the hard way and still 'religious' in the old-fashioned sense they had been through the war and tested their objective belief in the crucible of experience. Hence they placed freedom so highly and saw no contradiction between freedom and Christian belief. But the weakness of their position could not be concealed. They worked and wrote for a public which reads, and which, having read, argues, agrees, disagrees; in short, they imagined a world still eager to be influenced by doctrinal statements. Hence they worked quite independently and yet according to the same norm, namely that of long, difficult, and very good books. For example, Rahner's *Theological Investigations* scrutinizes all Christian claims in the light of the Catholic tradition and modern insights. Lexica such as *Sacramentum Mundi* and the *New Catholic Encyclopaedia* even attempt to mediate highly technical learning to the world at large. The sweep of this doctrinal broom, unencumbered by worn-out rubbish, achieves a monumental reappraisal of truth. Balthasar's genius goes further afield and draws, for the first time, upon our whole literary and dramatic culture, not in order to judge and condemn, nor to engage in Christian propaganda, but to buttress doctrinal insights with aesthetic foundations.

I responded to the gradual appearance of these works as one responds to revelation itself. Could our darkness be pierced at last by an *aggiornamento* which did not concentrate on ecclesiastical politics but on new sources of inspiration and truth? Would now the day dawn when the vast richness of the past would not be kept out of the Christian life of the community? Would such a day ensure the victory of the Spirit over the institutional routine? Would Shakespeare and Calderón, for example, fertilize the ever-shrinking compass of the preachers' minds? I could see nothing but promise in those hectic days. The cultural richness and the religious truth must transform not only the Church but also the world.

This promise never died. But the *aggiornamento* never found its centre of gravity in the classical inheritance of beauty. The books, and the men of the books, may have lasting influence, but they cannot compete in immediate effect with the partisans. When the reactionaries react furiously, and when the revolutionaries press their demands, the 'middle' are not only squeezed but often perish in the cross-fire of opposing violence. One former Jesuit friend of mine, who, I believe, represents an important group, declared privately soon after Vatican II that he had more in common with Trotsky than with Kerensky. Kerensky, it may be remembered, was the moderate revolutionary who ended the rule of the Tsar in 1917 and whose own rule was terminated within a few months. The young are, of course, always extreme, but it remains questionable whether our age of revolution will be content with spiritual *aggiornamento*. The Marxist–Leninist wing of Catholics interprets renewal not in the terms of tradition, weeded and re-sown, but in Jeremiah's phrase of 'plucking up, tearing down, trampling on, destroying' before the build-up of the new collectivist Jerusalem.

16

DIMENSIONS OF CHRISTIAN EXISTENCE

Why do things happen, and why do they happen the way they happen? The question, raised earlier in my life, now threatens again the interpretation of our strange times. The Catholic *aggiornamento* lies now buried beneath piles of paper. But documents, reports, commentaries, etc., cannot disguise the upheaval, for which the word 'renewal' may not turn out to be aptly chosen. Vatican II was a turning-point, no doubt; but whither led the roads coming out of it? The inspired and learned leaders who prepared the Council have for the most part come away from it dispirited. This is not what they had wanted at all. The aged Maritain grumbled as the *Peasant from the Garonne*. Once again the original vision bore no resemblance to the actual outcome. The vulgar had scored a victory, the banal had defeated the glorious enterprise. How could Balthasar welcome the new liturgy with its lowest common denominator of popular get-together worship? How could Congar apply the word 'tradition' to formulae which others interpreted in a sense opposed to tradition? As Balthasar said in a little pamphlet, directed against Rahner, what happens when things become serious? This Church is not renewed at all, and Christian existence is sold to the world.

On the other hand, the young and radicals protest against the minimal scope of renewal. Have things changed at all? Is not family planning still suspect? Is not the philosophy of 'Breed and multiply' the same mixture as before? How do the Church's treasures stand up in the age of mass starvation? Where is the promised freedom? Though the index of prohibited books no longer operates as before, do the authorities really encourage free inquiry and untrammelled dialogue? The ecumenical understanding limps along. And the authorities are answerable to no one but to themselves. How can there be justice without accountability, responsibility without representative procedure and elections? Such questions breed discontent and mistrust. Küng stands not alone as a Catholic who would give the *aggiornamento* a new twist towards radical reform.

The question why all this has happened and how it came to pass matters a great deal, for it bears also on the future. Christian existence ends if human beings are merely tossed around by their environment, and the *aggiornamento* can claim no exception. If it is only a milestone in social advance, yielding to economic pressures, it will also be devoured by these impersonal forces.

By 1960 I had learnt enough of the irony of history. The course of events never seemed to go the way it had been planned. The great resolutions and high-sounding treaties were soon forgotten. If you could not ratify a lasting peace for the world why were you more likely to find a Christian *scheme* which could define God and the world? If the United Nations, as became apparent, were becoming an institutionalized instrument of oppression, why look to historical developments as the stage on which truth would be manifested? True, I also had been brought up on Schiller's dictum that world-history is a kind of moral tribunal (*Weltgeschichte ist das Weltgericht*), and during the battles of Britain, Stalingrad, and Alamein, I did not find it hard to persuade myself that world-history was a rough guide to universal morality. But such a positive attitude became stickier as we approached the new barbarism. It could be that the whole spiritual reform since the war, far from articulating the ideal, constituted an anti-utopia. I became increasingly sure that the providential City of God had nothing to do with official pronouncements but everything with the apparently incidental bonuses, not at the centre but on the periphery of events.

Looking at history this way, one can sever the gold from the dross. Dante, the exile, for example, could not have become the author of the *Comedy* without the chaotic and evil turmoils of Florence around 1300. Our own age abounded with genius which flourished not in accordance with the state of society, but against it. The great men who prepared Vatican II had not worked in vain: their work will stand up for ever. And women, for the first time, can be heard above the welter of men's debating. Simone Weil, for example, would never have been heard of if the Dominican whom she consulted had not thought fit to tell the world about her after her death in England in 1943. Here was a Jewess, an intellectual who worked on the conveyor-belt at the Renault car factory, who became a Christian without submitting to baptism, who identified Christ with self-giving and humiliation and prophetically embodied the Servant Church. Her *Waiting on God* became a kind of spiritual manual, especially for those who felt the despair of *Waiting for Godot*, spelt out in Beckett's classic of 'the bastard — he does not exist'. Simone Weil championed the cross at a time when we longed to affirm life. Some of her railings against the God of the Old Testament irritated me beyond measure, but her contribution to the science of the cross came at the right time, when affluence seemed to flood Christian consciousness. With Edith Stein she has secured a Jewish stake in the dying of Christ and the world.

Women had, of course, always held a high place in the Christian scheme of things. The Blessed Virgin Mary had been the focus of devotion. Even Dante's Beatrice and other blessed ladies had taken their light from her who reflected the Eternal. The god-bearing and mediating Virgin Mother had even to a certain extent taken the place of God, if only because she stood for mild gentleness. Goethe, the non-Catholic, had ascribed to her the universal accessibility: all could come to her in trust. But the development in Christian thought and organization had been given over to men. Even Protestant theology, though free from monastic domination, was so male-oriented that the reader never even noticed how one-sided the style and content were. The fifty years of my life were politically and culturally in the hands of men, and the Pope's claim for Mary's share in the redemption of mankind did not avail at all. The *aggiornamento* triggered off and completed a tremendous vacuum. In many countries the Virgin Mother simply disappeared, and with it seemed to go the last vestige of motherly care, bridal romance, sisterly mirth. And yet running against the official stream we were given the works of women like Weil and Stein which drew not upon abstract formulations of doctrine but set forth the science of the cross from within their own experience, shared by millions of women.

This emergence of blessed ladies cannot be grouped with, or explained as, part of the women's liberation movement. The latter asserted its rights and fought for power, but the great spiritual women of this age gave their testimony for God against secular power. They did not even aspire to high office in religious orders or hospitals. Whenever it has been my good fortune to meet these new flowers of Francis or Clare I have felt them to be a revelation of self-giving, humorous, and competent love in a harsh world of claims and competition. They were not interested in statistics or resolutions, but they cared for people 'face to face'. I had never understood the Christian doctrine of forgiveness and the practice of prayer until I learnt of Edith Stein's martyrdom which culminates in her intercessory work for her murderers. From the example of Frau Rathenau to her day and beyond we have to turn to the loving face of such ladies, who in deepest grief impart the heavenly splendour to their surroundings. Balthasar's circle in Basel had experienced this under the aegis of Adrienne von Speyer, a doctor and theologian, but primarily a mystical servant of Christ. Cicely Saunders, founder of St Christopher's Hospice in South London, had brought to dying the dignity and hope of life in Christ. Mother Teresa's work in Calcutta became known the world over. Thus women have responded to the Spirit when the statues of our Lady were dismantled.

At the other end of the scale was a prophet who shone so brightly that his star must needs vanquish all our fears. His prophecies were as wrong as he was brilliant. Yet he was not a false prophet. Teilhard de Chardin, whose main work was done before he became known — he died in New York on Easter Sunday 1955 — appealed to us partly because his work had been suppressed by his own Jesuit order. He had been a victim of censorship, and that was almost enough to acclaim his vindication. But even more beguiling was his face, a firm, radiant, compassionate, even heroic mien, which expressed all one's hopes in a dismal world. His pen was a ready writer of these hopes. Instead of loading his pages with tiresome clichés of theology, such as eschatology, he released these theological terms from their prison house and let them run riot in his digs and scientific papers. The young stretcher-bearer priest, whom the slaughter of the First World War had not destroyed in any way, and who had gone to China in the wake of archaeological enterprises, soon to become the pioneer of new ones in the Gobi desert, told a tale very different from that of Simone Weil. It was a story of Christ-centred progress, a saga of cosmic advance, a gospel of universal and corporate newness in the leap from beginnings to the end. Teilhard also put the condition of man in the centre of his investigations, but this condition was not constrained by miserable crosses. Teilhard proclaimed the marvellous mutation, the evolution of the spiritual from the molecular, the making of the Christocentric reality in the consciousness of man. It seemed to me that Platonism was reborn in Christian guise, no longer floating on ideas, but buttressed by skeletons from the past and firmly controlled by spades and laboratories. The palaeontologist dug up the past to create the future, not as the pedants of the libraries and universities, but as the careful observer of a divine experiment of the creation. Hence Teilhard could talk of a *milieu divin* and give us a mass untied from liturgical texts and ecclesiastical walls.

I ignored the criticisms which inevitably followed the belated publication of his works. One would expect his order to utter muted protests against his theology, which seemed to leave out of account both the fall of man and his redemption. This accusation was easy to deal with, for his letters demonstrated his aristocratic awareness of the sinfulness of the world and his deliberate conquest of it. Here was not a man to wail or join the chorus of ineffectual lamentations, but a soldier who mastered his own temptations, especially the loneliness of his own heart. The *Letters from a Traveller* proved to my satisfaction that no one could have been more aware of the possibility of total failure. What could be more touching than this genius's constant reiteration: *Il faut bien finir*?

A good finish for oneself is one thing, but a good finish for the human race quite another. One should have heeded some of the savage criticism offered by Monod or Medawar,[1]

[1] Cf. *The Art of the Soluble*, 1967, pp. 71-81.

who attacked this Christian evolutionism with their own anti-Christian bias. But in the mid-fifties there was every reason to embrace Teilhard's prospect of an emerging humanity, which would, as it were, choose its own mutation. I, for one, wanted it to be true, and somewhat naively painted my own picture of what this human race would look like. Teilhard made us all into utopians and revived a utopian philosophy which would somehow use modern technology without submitting to it.

This human race, getting nearer the point of consummation called omega, would distil a state of consciousness from which it would exclude its lower destructive urges. We would no longer compete in order to destroy, but we would collaborate in order to survive on this higher plane. Science and the arts would naturally absorb and also regenerate our energies, so that new peaks of knowledge would be climbed. Work would be the harmonious foundation for the common enjoyment of these fruits of learning. One had visions of all our peoples studying, playing, planting, exploring, and also caring for one another. Here was the famous Republic of science, the Academy which knew no barriers of class, sex, creed, or race.

Nor was this utopianism quite lacking in factual potential. We were already becoming aware of the uncomfortable over-crowding on our little planet. The statistics which emerged from the United Nations sounded ominous. I remember a colleague's lecture in the department of geography which preceded the subsequent fashion of doom-watch. Prof. Pugh revealed the graphs relevant to actual population growth and predicted the figures for the sixties. The picture was utterly alarming. The gently rising curve suddenly became intoxicated and pointed vertically to the sky. Every inch of this vertical line signified the births and needs of millions. The ecological disaster was round the corner and the pressure on our resources promised strife rather than accord.

Teilhard's Utopia, as we interpreted it, seemed then to answer precisely to the threatened cul-de-sac, for if we could open the road to the stars — first the planets, then other systems — there would be no problem at all regarding surplus populations. On the contrary, these new beings, which had already opted for the mutation, would be the ideal travellers of the stars. Gagarin's flight in Sputnik I coincided nicely with these notions. Perhaps it was even part of the providential design that human beings should now colonize the universe and spiritualize the inert mass of matter.

Teilhard's idealism was underpinned by exhibits from the past and an analysis of the biological framework. He was neither a philosopher nor a theologian, but succeeded in comprehending the world as a scientist. He projected his self-effacing heroism into the universal expectation. Not many years passed before this expectation was punched and deflated like a worn-out balloon. Space-travel lost its practical potential as a way out of our earth problems. The human race showed no inclination for a move forward. The narrowest materialism made nonsense of the spiritualization of man. Yet there remained from Teilhard a legacy. When his scientific papers have entered the limbo of all such papers and his theories have been forgotten his poetic vision of man as the meaning of the universe will continue to inspire a disenchanted audience. He opposes the fragmentation of man into little units, disconnected organisms, which move through minute segments of reality, such as time and space. Teilhard revives that classical spectrum of an eternal, infinite, dynamic entity, which becomes a universe through the spiritual participation of the God-man. He can, therefore, shrug off the easy scorn of the empiricist, who exposes his claims to the blight of temporal setbacks or even momentous catastrophes. What are such setbacks and catastrophes, asks the disciple of Teilhard, except parochial aberrations?

This way of questioning makes us all into actors on the universal stage, and I linked Teilhard with the drama of Job. Once again one was compelled to acknowledge that all answers depend upon one's own point of view. Either one may, like Job, despair of world, friends, and self, because one suffers from the sickness unto death, or one may, also like Job, console oneself, not with finding God, but with one's creaturely submission to the majesty of Being. Teilhard also insisted, as does the divine answer in the book of Job, that the facts of life are sufficient as an answer to the human predicament. Perhaps the decisive human contribution to the universe is the conscious, deliberate, and grateful opening of eyes and ears, to formulate for oneself the simple question: 'Where were you when I made the stars?' The modern Job, as Teilhard showed us, is not confined to his natural eyes and ears, but has at his disposal the latest instruments of research. After Teilhard a veritable race in space exploration exploited new ways of measuring 'black holes', 'quasars', 'pulsars', and even more mysterious immensities. Given this background, who could doubt that Teilhard's main thesis was vindicated, namely, that we are here on a speck of dust in order to become the conscious migrants, from alpha to omega? All the old categories of judgement, our optimism and our pessimism, seemed to be overtaken by the wordless beyond.

Gradually I perceived that, as in antiquity and as in Dante's day, we were confronted with a universe of many, perhaps endless, dimensions. The complexity of our time, with its surplus of tearful incidents, seemed to have squashed the harmony of the spheres, and we moved as one-dimensional creatures on the surface of things. Like flies on window-panes we crawled, unable to get into the air and to the light. The lucky ones could add one or two dimensions to their daily routine, such as family life, or sport, or entertainment. But Christianity was meant to liberate us from the cave of our existence, and for some reason which I still could not define it had failed to do so. Then it dawned upon me that our theology was itself a victim of one-dimensional boredom, and that it was no accident that the renewal came from so many obscure and unexpected quarters. The great ladies and Teilhard were an earnest of more to come. One might almost say that the greater the oppression of the world the vaster the opening of new spiritual dimensions must be. Here was a dialectic quite contrary to the all-conquering Marxist–Leninist materialism. Whereas they calculated in material quantities, of which the human classes were a part, the real dialectic of truth pointed to qualitative distinctions of immeasurable possibilities.

At this time Tillich's *Systematic Theology* appeared in three volumes (1953–64). He had proved, as already mentioned, his political mettle during the years of resistance against Hitler and his support for Roosevelt. I gasped when my own tentative findings found more than an echo in his model of Being and beings. He has, of course, also been criticized for his use (and abuse?) of such categories as Being, which are dangerous because vague. For example, what is the good of talking about 'the Ground of our Being', which then became a cliché, just like Tillich's concept of 'ultimate concern' as something approaching God? But details did not, and do not, worry me. Tillich related our world, as we experienced it on complex and inter-weaving levels, to the Christian tradition, and in doing so demonstrated a multi-dimensional awareness of both. I could now at last understand how you can be sickened by one aspect of religion or work or family, and yet also be devoted to, and in need of, all these. Tillich simply articulated what every mature man and woman must realize sooner or later, namely, that you cannot reduce human existence to a common denominator, and that every human problem craves for a transcending level of response. We are alienated from our true state, and history is the index of our alienation; but we also long for acceptance, and the spiritual dimension of history is our concern.

Theologians will shake their heads at my findings and murmur the indictment, 'syncretism'. But I defy the threat, since I no longer seek to belong, or try to believe in, any school, whether ideological or theological. I seem to want the best of all worlds: a Barthian Christ-centred revelation, a cosmic-scientific mysticism associated with Teilhard, a multi-dimensional cultural correlation as popularized by Tillich. Is this possible? The question is not academic only, nor even answered by the personal gulf which Barth, for example, summarized in his acceptance of Tillich as a charming man (which, following his wife's disclosures, seems a strange evaluation) and a champion of impossible notions in theology. No, our history forces upon us an interpretation of its own text, and this text is so paradoxical that anything less than a revelatory source from above, a scientific scrutiny of our materials at hand, and an artistic apprehension of our state, must fail in providing light in the dark, and shade in the glittering scene. Either a total silence, or a veritable chorus in polyphony, meet the challenge — or, better still, a silence interwoven with the celestial spheres.

17

THE DIVINE COMEDY

My debt to Dante and Goethe needs little stressing after the previous chapters. The *Divine Comedy* and *Faust*, in particular, have never ceased to inspire me with the conviction that our generation, too, is on the move, and that I must despite all the appearances to the contrary find a way through the endless obstacles and layers which impede the pilgrimage. My progress began in 1934, in the Italian Hospital in London, when under an anaesthetic, given for the removal of my tonsils, I had a vision of the truth in which my light was suffused with the light of circles of love which converged upon the centre from which they took their origin. Little did I know then that this gift was an intimation of the beatific vision and that my happiness belonged to the realm from which I was then yet excluded. I had not heard of Isaiah and Ezekiel, and the Transfiguration of Jesus in the company of Moses and Elijah had not entered my sphere of learning. It took many years to trace my experience back to the mystical tradition which receives its final imprint in Dante's *Paradiso*. But the ascent had begun. Baptism, Confirmation, Ordination paved the way.

It ended in 1963. We were having guests for dinner on 22 November 1963 when my daughter came down in pyjamas to tell us — did we know? President Kennedy had been shot in Dallas, Texas. A few minutes later she reappeared. Kennedy was dead. The next three days I spent in hell, in as far as tears, shock, indignation, and prayer can be held to pertain to the apex of despair. All the previous acts of violence, all the currents of resentment, envy, and violence, which had in the past cast doubt on all my hopes, seemed to flow into the scene of horror, conveyed to us meticulously by reporters and pictures. Was I any wiser than in the early days when Rathenau had been 'knocked off'? Could I tolerate the grief more easily? Could the Comedy still continue if a high-velocity rifle with a telescopic lens could silence for all time the very symbol of youth, courage, and enterprise? I was certainly not alone in breaking my heart. Millions all over the world, who knew the man as little as I did, mourned and could not be comforted. Our bereavement was personal, but it was also ideological. The cynical voice of Mark Antony spoke as from within:

> Now let it work: mischief, thou art afoot
> Take thou what course thou wilt![1]

Why had we ever expected relief from fire? Why should the conspirators cease their game of murder? Why should the powerful abstain from pricking the names of their victims? The religious and sociological climate had cast a mantle of deceit over the earthly scene. What we had wanted, and nearly obtained, was a human comedy. In such a comedy we would outgrow the monstrous past. Yet the egregious Walter Ulbricht of my youth ruled in the German Democratic Republic without repentance of any sort. In Hungary Cardinal Mindszenty escaped from prison only to seek refuge in the American embassy. All over the Communist world the grip of collectivism stengthened and the dreary destiny of mankind became fixed. The alienation of man had become institutionalized, and though the villains departed (Serov, Beria, for example) new ones stepped into their office. They could not abolish death, but they ended the springs of new life.

This lowest dimension of existence, which extends its tentacles into every corner of life, has no face. It is meaningless, for it seeks no meaning. Yet we cannot get rid of it as if it were nothing. Its power is that of a cancer. It is not content with the death it administrates but it lusts after the absorption of healthy tissues. I came to see that bureaucratic collectivism is not only wasteful economically and stifling culturally but agressively demonic. This Marxist–Leninist theory spells out its circles of hell in our times just as Dante's *bolge* mapped the anti-dimensions of life in the Middle Ages. The anti-norms of humanity describe the descent into total slavery.

[1] *Julius Caesar* III. 2, 265-6.

The controlling motivation behind this cancerous growth is individual envy and resentment. The collective becomes the open-armed breeding ground for the lazy, untalented, cruel, cowardly miscreant. A career is assured of success in proportion to its ruthless designs. Thus, as in Dante's time, the individual devils give a mask of reality to their demonic chaos and fragmentation. Our *Inferno* only differed in degree from that of the *Divine Comedy*. The appearances of the masks altered the tone of the comedy, too. Alas, verse was no longer appropriate to these prosaic characters.

Vyshinsky (1883-1954) remains my favourite representative of the modern demonic. When I listened to his denunciations at the United Nations, where he served as the Soviet Union's chief delegate, I could not but tremble. When I scrutinized this face of one whom Harold Laski had once called the 'ideal Minister of Justice' I registered the power of fascination once ascribed to the serpent. This Polish ex-Menshevik, who as judge and prosecutor had somehow survived the purges of the NKVD, wore the mask of the total rottenness of his world. In the trials of the 'anti-Soviet Trotskyist centre' in 1937 he had served Stalin well. Later he played a prominent part in the Sovietization of Latvia and Rumania. This little official of the brutal and sarcastic manner had sent thousands to their death on charges as empty as the fictional evidence squeezed out of tortured throats. All this belonged to the past, in which my own brother also had perished. But what troubled me above all was the inexplicable fact that this opportunist, turned Bolshevik only after Lenin's triumph, achieved in New York an air of acceptability: 'the hideous man not only was spared, but went on to new honours in diplomacy'.[1] Obituaries referred to his agreeable humour when off duty. Thus this 'rat in human form', this 'gangland lawyer'[2] has entered history books on the same mild level as Stalin's 'mistakes'.[3] When he died no one denounced this servile coward, the quasi-academic lawyer who had decimated his own faculty of law in Moscow.

---

[1] Cf. Adam B.Ulam, *Stalin*, 1974, p.424.
[2] Cf. Robert Conquest, *The Great Terror*, 1968, pp.17, 506.
[3] Cf. Roy A. Medvedev, *Let History Judge*, 1972, *passim*.

The condemnation of Vyshinsky does not ask for Miltonic verse, for this cold monster can only be classified in the jargon of administrative prose. Yet Ulam is right when he concludes that the Soviet terror is not incidental, but central to an essentially religious ideology. The victims 'died so that life should prove the truth of dogma'. The terror was the means of making men believe in the dogma, and the dogma appealed to the 'universal religious existentialist craving in human nature'.[1] Dostoyevsky had already sketched this demonic aspect in the novel *The Devils*, where Stavrogin has a hold over the murderers as Lucifer over the tools of the inferno. Koestler, too, had explained in his *Darkness at Noon* how it came about that the old faithful confessed, and wanted to confess. Their innocence had to be sacrificed to the guilt of the system, and this system they could not deny. Bodies and minds were tortured and broken so that this dogma might be feared and acknowledged. The hideous strength of the lie recalls the Beast of the Apocalypse, which must pounce and devour. Vyshinsky, theologically speaking, is the devil within a Satanic dream of power, and though dead, he and his line are not extinct.

Dante's circles of hell are well defined and symbolized by the jeering and horrendous monsters. In their defiance they manifest an almost heroic brutishness. Similarly Mozart's Don Giovanni descends into the flames with a certain grandeur of evil, the seducer seduced and unrepentant. But our top jailers possess not a whiff of heroism. Himmler and Vyshinsky belong to the world of Kafka's *Castle*, civil servants with dossiers, chauffeurs and messengers, porters and barmen. Hence only prose can do justice to their prosaic emptiness. The vast literature which has sprung up since the war translates the nightmare into narrative. The tormentors keep their silence and, like Iago at the end of *Othello*, 'never will speak word'. They come to me in my dreams, staring at me from still photographs of the kind taken of a class at school or a year at college. Clean-shaven or bearded, in uniform or civilian dress, they peer out of their masks to boast of their former careers. My contemporaries, too, see and hear them

[1] Ulam, op. cit., p.740.

145

in their dreams, still sniggering at their routine successes, though intimidated by their superiors. Fear and mistrust pertain to these officials, dehumanized by the system which they have made and sustained.

Alexander Solzhenitsyn's genius has not only nailed the socialist lie as a political monstrosity, but he has portrayed its spiritual failure. In his *First Circle* human beings act out even unwittingly aspects of truth which the lie cannot contain. The author shares with the reader the implicit conviction that the First Circle implies not only the existence of even deeper circles of torment, but also that of circles which lead upward and beyond, towards a human existence redeemed and set free from the system. The *First Circle* is not a political tract, but, like the rest of Solzhenitsyn's work, stands in the classical literary tradition, brought up to date, accusing and liberating. From within the camp there arises in letters of blood the eternal theme of humanity which bursts the wires and walls. This assertion of freedom is spiritual evidence against the validity of socialist collectivism and for the unending truth of human destiny, unfettered, beyond conditioning, made perfect in suffering.

This interpretation of our era transcends the limits of historical existence. Just as the Greek tragedians reconcile us to necessity, and as the Christian writers make sinners happy culprits, and as Dante ascends through circles of stench and filth to the light of the blessed stars, as Shakespeare leads us from blasted heath, murder, treachery, and every conceivable ill to the clear air, as Goethe attains peace for the Faustian blind, so do the Russian writers unmask the lie and rediscover the undying truth of the freedom of Spirit.

I saw that Kennedy's death was politically a disaster, but spiritually an affirmation of the Divine Comedy. Kennedy belonged to those who 'encounter darkness as a bride',[1] though they seemed destined for the full sheaves of harvest. Shakespeare authorizes a preference for death free from all mawkish morbidity. Ours is no suicidal frivolity, for our flesh rejects the cold, rotting, viewless clod. But for millions the terror of the murderers makes death better than life.

[1] Measure for Measure III. 1,82. This scene sums up all the pros and cons regarding death.

Claus Bonhoeffer, Dietrich's brother, epitomized the feelings of my generation when he welcomed his moment of release, saying: 'Not to see these faces any more!' I could now see that, from the least to the greatest, men could, without being saints, achieve life in death. They were martyrs in our century over whom one could repeat the marvellous incantation:

> Fear no more the heat o' the sun,
> Nor the furious winter's rages

for they had suffered the frown of the great and were past the tyrant's stroke, gone home with their wages.[1]

The eschatological dimension, therefore, dominates the evaluation of our period as that of any other. If death takes all, then men have been fooled and the whole passing scene is a joke, a tease of the kind which Hardy credits to the Omnipotent with playing from behind the wings.[2] If the dead are not raised Auschwitz stands for the essencē of man's hopeless case. But if the gassed are not slain for ever, but rise as a mighty army, we are not only consoled for our loss but confront the collectivist tyrannies with the total reversal. The one word *Resurrexit* interprets history as none other. Whereas death is always the final threat of the oppressor life is the vindication of the oppressed which terminates the oppressor's rule.

Kennedy's death compelled me to reassess all the old arguments for life after death. I found them cumulatively convincing, but their association with experiments quite distasteful. Case histories of messages, automatic writing, or other intimations of survival seemed to me no more relevant to our theme than the twitchings of an eel in the frying-pan in postmortem muscular movements. Clearly the Divine Comedy of our time must counter the 'nothing' of modern nihilism with more than continuance.

If existence in human history amounts to alienation, continuance is the last thing to look for. Dante solved the problem as a Christian. He makes his escape from hell through knowledge (Virgil), motivated by love (Beatrice), made

---

[1] *Cymbeline*, IV.2, 258ff.
[2] *Tess of the D'Urbervilles*, last paragraph.

effective by repentance in the ascent through purgatory. The grim masks threaten, but have no more power. Oblivion and renewal give perspective to history: a very little thing, down below, a testing ground for eternity in the stars. Thus alienation ends in mystical contemplation through the reflection of God. Goethe, too, while retaining a realistic this-worldly credo, sees history as a parable, for the transitory is overtaken by the lasting, and the reflection serves the light in myriad colours. Dostoyevsky in the *Brothers Karamazov* accentuates the choice between the alienated and those who desire integration: Ivan, honest and clever, 'hands back his ticket' in disgust with the cruel world, but Alyosha, immature and passionate, abandons self in loving service, thus saying 'yes' to the world. Thomas Mann also sees love, the loving disposition, at the heart of the problem of the human sanatorium, where — in *The Magic Mountain* — all are sick and most want to be sick, a few die against their will, and none achieve health. Love itself is questionable, for without love we cannot live, and yet we kill and are killed by love. 'Can we ever love again?' is the haunting question in this century.

The youth of Kennedy's America played with these possibilities of escape from history, and soon Europe, too, was in the grip of the new culture. I first heard of hippies in San Francisco as a totally new phenomenon. But when they spread their wings and reached the old Continent I saw that they were translating fiction into fact through customary means. Drugs and togetherness, ecstasy and irresponsibility, rebellion against conventions, sexual freedom, religious cults characterized the movement. My children imported a version of this explosive 'yes' and 'no' to life into our home. Unfortunately it shook the house with the vibration of the pop music, which, though also not new, exceeded previous rock with a degree of noise which only modern electronic amplifiers could produce.

This outburst of a pampered generation in self-induced ecstasy did not serve the Divine Comedy despite its religious content. Yet it stressed the strains of a generation which questioned its own identity. Its search for the wisdom of the East, pursued often with pathetic ignorance, proved the bankruptcy of established Christendom. Their fascination with *karma* and *nirvana* negated the secularization of theology. If the Christian God was dead, or near-dead, they could not be blamed for opting out of society, even if the road to Katmandu led nowhere.

The protest stands for something like repentance. It mocks at yachts and private planes, colour supplements, and wants to stem the tide of ecological disaster. It repudiates bigness and no longer despises little. Thus a return of the utopian ideal crowns years of wasteful expansion. This ideal is opposed to corporate power. It is immature, because it is young and mixes, as the early Christian communities, an otherwordly individualism with social concerns. If the groups and cells which experiment with the making of true community fail they are nevertheless to be hailed as pilgrims on the road.

Kennedy's children fared badly physically and spiritually. From Haight-Ashbury came the junkies with sad songs, from Vietnam spread mournful defeat. We had reached the watershed. Security, mortals' chiefest enemy, had bred insecurity. We had come a long way from before 1914 to the day Kennedy died. Now false prophets were exposed. Reforms could no longer halt the Gadarene descent. What followed in the sixties was predictable, for we were spiritually engulfed in the pouches of our false desires. It seemed to me that the Divine Comedy had become what it had been from the start: a cruel farce.

18

THE FINAL TASK

Jaundice, or rather infective hepatitis, is a diabolical disease. I caught it from the children who caught it at school from a recently arrived Pakistani child. They got over it lightly, but I suffered not only days of delirium but also the genuine horrors of hell. Jaundice allows you no respite: day and night, hour by hour, every minute, you go through the agony of existence. The delirium of a high fever brings the blackest darkness. You gather up in yourself all the poison dormant and active in yourself and, as it seems, in the world around you. You hate to be seen, but you loathe to be left alone. As you grow more yellow and your appearance mocks at the human face, a slight alleviation succeeds to the intense terror. Not having died — for which you prayed, but in vain, for in England people generally survive the disease though no cure is known — you experience next total exhaustion. You still cannot eat, nor can you read or listen. You are still in hell, for now your mind registers even more distinctly the shadings of nausea. Nothing matters, says your mind; nothing survives, tells your voice; nothing can come out of this, you conclude. All the hells are let loose again at night. Interminable seems the wakeful stretch of time, for it is now time itself which seems to control the torment. Into this time wander the images of despair. You are forsaken, you are for ever shut up in yourself, in your toxic bloodstream. You are forsaken like Troilus, deserted, betrayed, unloved; you are closeted in the prison, like Sartre's characters. You are the treason and the prison. You cannot love God or wife or children. They have all left you.

Then, one day, in a warm season of early spring, you see the light as the curtains are drawn. You can now bear the light. You peer through the window, from your bed, in great weakness. You see that the bare trees have a green sheen about them. There are buds on the branches of the lightest hue. Can the tree live again? Tears well up and, like the dew, they water the inner desert. You hear the voice of the woman you love. A smiling child holds out a hand. The doctor looks in, as he has done every day, and says: 'You have turned the corner'. You consume a morsel of food, you are washed, you shave in bed. Weeks pass, you rise, and you are slowly re-made. You can listen to Mozart again. You take courage and you hope in him who has been absent for so long. But you are not what you were before. You need not be told to refrain from alcohol and greasy food. You are chastened for ever. Life is now held on a lease, and it is treasured anew. The remembrance of inner pollution can never yield again to pride or achievement. And the history of the times somehow looks different.

At the end of these fifty years I obtained as a prize that inner detachment which gives you distance. No longer the cheating detachment, which I willed in adolescence, but an imposed detachment. You no longer live to yourself or want to live to yourself, for in this inner detachment you are freed toward all that is not self. From it springs the distance from events. You know its dangers. If, for you, 'all the world's a stage' you are looking for masks and not for reality. Distance may utter still 'nothing mattered, nothing matters; all things have passed, are passing'. But distance may yield the proper perspective as a protection, and it came to me as a bonus after jaundice.

Even without jaundice sick humanity longs for this distance, for without it the fragmentation around us becomes the fragmentation within. The former resistance fighter who confesses now: 'It was not worth it — I should never do it again' (meaning: hiding the innocent, running endless risks, waiting, waiting...) can only compare the past with the present. He sees the victims and hears their anguished cries; then he watches the stupid and evil generation of his sons, lifts his shoulders, shakes his head, and lapses into the negative creed: I do not believe in the meaning of the past. But, given the distance, he passes over from his narrow remembrance to the universal circles. Hence our history must include all the triumphs on the stage, music, films, books which, in their several ways, have opened dimensions and

151

recesses, making for us a large room.

The Marx Brothers' *A Night at the Opera* eternalizes this distance, as applicable to our time. Drama and passion are played out on the stage, with Groucho making love to the formidable lady; but behind the scenes Harpo hangs on the ropes which work the props, and the scene changes from battleships to rose-gardens, while the lady goes on singing. The interpreter of our history looks at the stage, identifies with the actors, changes the scenery, and laughingly assesses the fragmentary comedy which he has superimposed upon the cast.

As an interpreter I take up my position not only at the theatre but at airports or railway stations. There is constant movement. Faces emerge and vanish. Crises of sorts occur. Nationalities, different age groups, men and women, rich and poor, all the 'multitudes in the valley of decision', as Joel calls them, pass by. They are history in its fragmentary nuclear form. But their now is hedged by their past and also by their future.

For the Russian novelists the railway station is the hub of all the contradictions of life, and it still remains the same. Here is a solid foundation which lives for movement. Here trains arrive and leave quite impersonally, and here the most intense greetings and farewells begin or end countless destinies. Zürich Hauptbahnhof is enshrined in my memory as the sorting house of our historical chaos, for here all the members of my family made their decisions for life or death. Most of my generation in Europe came off or boarded trains here, and as they glided out an inexorable turning-point had been reached. No train goes *through* Zürich: it must turn round. So also most of the heroes of these memories came in and went out, for only a few ever came to stay. How to compound freedom with necessity may be learnt by spending hours, especially at night, amidst the shining lights and signals, studying the indicators, and watching the stream of humanity, in and out. On the platform of Zürich station I can see Thomas Mann and his family, exiled first, then returning vindicated, but still questioning: 'Can love ever arise again?' Einstein is another invisible ghost, for in this city and on these platforms he must have reflected on relativity well before the catastrophe of war. Here Joyce declaimed *Ulysses* to himself, and at the same time, during the First World War, Busoni walked up and down with music as his companion, night by night. Here also came Hesse, who explored the demonic before it struck its deadly assault, and meditated on the two irreconcilable ways of sensuality and discipline.

From the distance all the paradoxes can be seen. They can no more be understood than a good picture. I can see, divided by only two centuries (or even less), how the child Mozart comes to Zürich, already a miracle, full of grace, and, before the railways, enduring the travel by coach; and Lenin, working away at Bolshevik policy and sensing victory even before it is achieved. And I can hear the paradox of our history, as I listen to the C-minor Mass of the former, a torso full of darkness and light, and the latter's epoch-making oratory which shook the world.

Distance does not resolve the paradox of the past, but it gives it a new direction. Just as the trains arrive and leave again, so I begin to perceive that my story has not been about what has been, but about what is yet to be. The lines lead in from the past, and they lead out into the future. This is the supreme paradox of history in time, for we do not stand still. A Mozart must die soon after his travels across Europe, and a Lenin only rules for a few years after the revolution. But their work lives on. It touches the nerve centre of our existence. We also are part of what is yet to be. Hence we must observe Dante's advice: *E voi mortali, tenetevi stretti a giudicar.* . . . The end is not yet, and we must judge with restraint.

Through the distance and with restraint we can now apprehend through the paradox how it came about, what it was, and what it will be in the future. The flaw of our times lies in the past and in our common humanity. Boredom and demonic ability combined to construct an empire, to which all contributed in the mistaken notion that it would yield material happiness. The Faustian enterprise to create the world of superman degenerated into the vast administrative collectivism which acknowledges no spiritual destiny now or ever. Its main principle of envy and meanness disguises its demonic character. Its spokesmen refer to themselves as 'reasonable men'. Yet they are digging the grave of their own material culture. I can now see in one huge sweep the battlefields of the first war, the extermination camps of the second, the atom bombs which fell and which will explode with hydrogen nuclear fission and multi-war heads, directed and homing to targets with cybernetic controls, either straight from silos on earth, or submarines, or satellites in the air. This will end the ecological rape of the planet which the parasites have conquered. Our history has only advanced the apocalyptic scourge. It began before us and it will consume the world after us, but within measurable time. It is rendered possible by the technological inventions of our era. It is made necessary by the spiritual degradation, in which the demonic has become split from the religious life of the people and runs its empty course. The apocalypse replies logically and emotionally to the spiritual betrayal which these pages have chronicled.

This apocalypse, however, has lost its poetic appeal. Nothing is left to the imagination as the scourges come over the world. Red horse, pale horse, black horse, riders on the horse, in the chariot, used to embellish war, famine, and death with an aura of awe. The biblical imagery lent the dimensions of meaning to the horrors of war. Here was vindication and even glory, culminating in the assertion that the pangs of the universe belong to the providential order. But even later in the modern age men of genius kept it up. Newton can never be cited for science alone, for Daniel and the apocalypse made up his universe of gravitation. Even after him, as the industrial age applied science, a secularized apocalypse still knitted a remarkably powerful winding-sheet for the oppressed. Who could be more evocative than Dickens of the apocalyptic dimension? Cemeteries, criminals, cruelties, elopements, drownings, fog, dirt, gloom, soot, grease, pinching poverty, wild nights, frost, starvation, shreds, shutters, coarse sacking, a candle guttered down, scum, mist, and neglect, foul and filthy air, faintness, a stale odour, gaunt eyes stare down upon the bed of death. All this is splendid, for Dickens still evokes an apocalyptic world which longs for liberation and which must achieve light, love, goodness, and life. No longer a victory of the Lamb, certainly, but still a victory, a framework of martyrdom and restoration. But look now at the Himmlers and Vyshinskys, their peers and successors, and you have an apocalypse of a civil service, a secret police, of *enfants terribles* (Cocteau). If they have control of the communications humanity is doomed, for all roads lead to perdition. The apocalyptic 'what is yet to be?' finds no echo, only a stupid, repetitive, taped, procedural order. Our historical apocalypse discloses nothing, reveals no one.

The distance of faith, however, grants us a reprieve. We look at the sleazy, slimy, creaking machine of destruction and put upon it a pattern of revelation. The apocalyptic, which no longer reveals anything, becomes Christian apocalypse through a total change of key. Since we view the present in the light of the past and in the expectation of the future we discover a centre of gravity, which is neither in the past, present, or future, but in the Person, Face, or Presence of God. We find ourselves in the long tradition of men and women who react to their condition by transforming *It* through calling upon, listening to, enjoying the *Thou*, the Other, God.

It is important to see this miraculous transformation not as an isolated eccentricity or even a common therapeutic exercise. The psalmist who calls for help, Job who cannot find 'Him', the fishermen who toil all night and take nothing until 'He' comes, Saul who is struck blind outside the gates of Damascus and hears the voice of accusation, the never-ending succession of martyrs who hope in that which they cannot see, Augustine who despairs of life and himself until he hears the 'Take up, and read', the Florentine poet who, deep in the dark wood of suicidal fantasies, descends with his guide to ascend to Him, Pascal, who exchanges the systematic knowledge of things for the God of Abraham, Isaac, and Jacob, Teilhard who espies the point Omega as the Christification of the world. . .all these men and women represent a formidable phalanx of visionaries who disclose the meaning of their history not as an external apocalypse, but as an internal revelation. They address the Presence face to face, and in the freedom of this address they are changed into his likeness. Thus metamorphosis, change of form and substance, out of history, comes to be seen as the meaning of history.

This metamorphosis can only be expressed in prayer to God. It rests upon the diapason of penitence and regret. The lament is its appropriate voice. A litany of modern fallen Jerusalems compiles itself: in our time the words of Wilfred Owen and the music of Benjamin Britten commemorate the immemorial theme. Sorrow and tears, with the restraint of formal composition, fuse in the choruses. The lamentation is about bereavement: 'How she sits solitary. . .' Every year and more often we remember 'them': the endless throng of victims, as they were shot, bombed, burnt, herded together, carried off, sorted, gassed, hanged, tortured. But they are now at peace, and as we lament their fate, with penitence and also with pride, a great transformation comes over the historical scene. The dead are no longer dead. Filled with pity our mourning transforms our vision. Pity yields to serene reconciliation, not yet with the murderers, but with the Presence, for we see that he is in their midst and was always among them. The Son of Man joins the children in the oven and our lamentation in which we cry *De profundis* reveals in the apocalyptic nothing the victor over guns, bombs, fires, transports, gas, and gallows. The whole tragic tradition of mankind finds its fulfilment in the cosmic elegy. Therefore the primary task of the Church, woefully neglected in these days of treachery, is to weep for the dead, to release fountains of tears, to enter spiritually the tombs and ovens. Then history is not merely stated, nor the organization of death-camps described, nor the villains pilloried, but the whole nightmare is transformed by the Spirit.

With the requiem for the world we reach the fine point of the intersection of history — secular and frightful — and the area beyond history — spiritual and consoling. This requiem is not escapist. In Mozart's *Requiem* the tears and the demonic blend in a dying man's last testament. Verdi presents us with the cacophony of legions of devils in the *Dies irae*. But even without these classical masterpieces we intone *Requiem aeternam* in the knowledge that these prayers are for real people. Significantly we do not pray for the rest of neutral institutions. They are dead. Nor do we intercede for armies, navies, air-forces. We do not plead for mercy on committees and all the wretched energies spent on the mismanagement of the world. There is in the requiem for the world a total negation of the impersonal. The solemnity is reserved for those who have passed through this history and whose souls have been touched by all the ambiguities of duty, guilt, neglect in the routine of their lives.

We add, therefore, to the long list of the known and the unknown the names of our period. The plural of the many gives place to the singular of the individual. The plea for the martyrs is easy for they deserve our prayers, and we make sense of their deaths through our prayers. Rathenau, Bonhoeffer, Kennedy head my list of many who have 'made history'. But the task of intercession does not stop there. Founders, benefactors, kinsfolk, dependents of all sorts also 'make history' when they are added to the scroll of remembrance. The problem is the enemy. 'Let us sleep now', says Wilfred Owen's 'enemy', and his enemies are united in rest eternal.

We have reached the crux of the matter. Given the distance and restraint, which we now practise, it would seem easier than before to 'pardon' the enemies. From the stars of Dante's *Paradiso*, and even through our telescopic lenses, the notorious evil-doers of our twentieth century seem small and empty, unworthy of attention. What is Himmler now? Why worry about Vyshinsky? But this attitude is truly 'gnostic' in the worst sense, for it blots out all distinctions. It also makes nonsense of the conflict of our time, which we believe to be somehow linked to an eternal and meta-historical reality. This treatment of the 'enemy' is certainly superficial and cosily suburban. It sentimentalizes lazily the supreme issues of our time. Furthermore, to consign Bonhoeffer and his hangmen to one 'eternal rest' induces that amoral disposition which bodes ill for the present and the future. If all come to the same end, namely a restful sleep without judgement, little is to be said for resistance at any time. The present and future perverters of the truth would have an easy time if we now declare that

157

murderers and murderered, tragic heroes and tragic victims, attain to the same port. This so-called universalism has indeed played havoc with our spiritual history. As I have shown, the hideous mistake of appeasement came out of a pacifism which misread reality, earthly and heavenly.

Yet we should deceive ourselves if we regarded this matter lightly. The 'love for the enemies' is so engrained in the Christian teaching that one can never wholly get rid of its paradoxical import. The very words 'love' and 'enemies' are locked in strife, and no natural harmony flows from the juxtaposition. The New Testament is an eloquent witness to the complexity arising out of this paradox. Even in the early Church we find opposing parties, and personal hostilities extend to the apostles themselves. They stand against each other 'face to face'. Principles are at stake and are fought out, as between Paul, Peter, and James. Indeed, no New Testament can be thought of apart from conflict and hostile dialectics. Nevertheless, these inner tensions cannot be compared to the persecutions from outside. Martyrs, it is true, forgive their killers and 'vengeance belongs to the Lord'. Thus Christians dilute and transform the ancient strain of revenge, which proceeded according to a moral calculus of compensation and retribution. But even such a transformation, made possible through detachment, distance, and restraint, cannot be thought of as 'love'. The love which converts the enemy is also known and gives rise to the belief that the blood of the martyrs is the seed of the Church.

These basic Christian tenets remain to this day, but they cannot be viewed in isolation. The whole Christian tradition oscillates between accusation and forgiveness, and the greatest Christians are both fighters and detached saints. There is no evidence that Athanasius loved Arius, or Hieronymus the followers of Origen, or Augustine his former Manichaean friends, the Donatists, or Pelagius, the good British monk. However, their lip-service to the divine love was by no means hypocritical. They loathed their enemies for the sake of God's love. They created thus an aggressive tradition by which they interpreted the history they suffered, and even Dante, so many centuries later, does not detract from this picture of a cosmic battle, in which he is his own worst enemy, ultimately forgiven through penitential progress, but where the real enemies cannot be forgiven, or loved, since their hatred is obdurate.

The problem still confounds our minds. We find ourselves in closest rapport to Milton, though we do not agree with his politics. For him the mythology of cosmic battles has already worn thin, but they are symbolic of the strife which goes on in every soul, and thence in society. With Milton we affirm the existence of the enemy, though we would take the sheen off the glitter of Lucifer and his angels. The old, blind Milton's *Samson Agonistes* comes nearest to our evaluation of our share in the evil and our liberation from the dreaded enemy.

The biblical narrative has never lost its pertinence, for it views the scene of conflict with involvement and detachment at the same time. Its hero is not a blameless man of virtue. He belongs to the wild world of passion and madness, though set apart for the service of God. He embodies all the strains of political confusion. Above all Samson remains pertinent to my theme for he represents the struggle of Israel. Eyeless in Gaza he even centres our attention on the Middle East and a very probable outcome of the stalemate there. As Samson dies and with him his tormentors, as he pulls down the pillars of their temple, he symbolizes the hopes and the fears of an apocalyptic age. Milton turns him into a tragic figure, perhaps *the* tragic figure, to interpret his own conflict of spirit and the agony of succeeding ages, including our own. In particular Milton makes no pious bones over the 'desolation of a hostile city'. The triumph over the 'slaughtered foes' — 'his enemies fully reveng'd' — unfolds the meaning of universal history, in which the noble perish.

Samson stands out as the ambiguous prototype of all helpless resistance against the worldly power. Samson is certainly paradoxical: elect — 'designed for great exploits' — and 'liable to fall'. Samson's fall lies within the highest dispensation. The loss of sight corresponds to the initial misapprehension of natural strength. The man has become the worm in a total eclipse — 'the sun to me is dark' — since the inner foes eased the way to the 'enemies who come to stare'. Affliction and insult from outside complete the humiliation suffered from within. For there is a split of personality in that the right will is separated from the pleasure principle. Abstinence is no guarantee by itself: the man who is betrayed by his sexuality has already betrayed his own strength.

This analysis at last explains why our high culture and learning have proved so ineffective against brute power during the years under review. The vessel was 'gloriously rigg'd' but the pilot too foolish to bring the ship home. Folly does not mean intellectual lack of insight, but failure of moral concentration. We were eroding our capital and opening the fortress to the Philistines. 'Just are the ways of God, and justifiable to men', once we grasp that we are part of the providential order. This order cannot be maintained without an active spiritual response on a massive scale. Samson's individualism and neglect of the community seals the doom. He goes into captivity, and his captors 'make sport'.

Milton recommends penitence as a cure, but it is not the penitence of a churchy kind: 'Repent the sin, but if the punishment thou canst avoid, self-preservation bids' The pardon here sought initiates a reformation of character which no longer despairs of life. Samson rightly asks: 'To what can I be useful, wherein serve my nation. . .'. As long as the enemy is 'let in', even if one gate is shut, nothing can be done. There is no ransom from the enemy. The therapy must be such as to heal the inner corruption, and there is the rub: 'God of our Fathers, what is man!' The religious answer must focus on this question, for there can be no godly intervention except in and through man.

Milton demonstrates that retrogression is not pardon. Delilah's appeal to let bygones be bygones cannot be accepted. Similarly, we should fool ourselves by granting a general pardon, thus obscuring the facts of the case. All the usual pleas of extenuating circumstances are, if allowed, stings of the serpent. What Milton calls 'female usurpation' may now be equated as the pleasure principle which must be resisted if Samson is to be re-made. The fight which ensues is with a giant, and the pedlar in pleasures and luxuries is now cast for a militant role:

> But come what will, my deadliest foe will prove
> My speediest friend, by death to rid me hence;
> The worst that he can give, to me the best.

After such a resolution we can join the chorus:

> Oh how comely it is, and how reviving
> To the spirits of just men long opprest,
> When God into the hands of their deliverer
> Puts invincible might, . . .

Samson quits himself like – Samson! So Milton's grand summing-up after the cataclysm of the 'dearly-bought revenge, yet glorious'. The tragic history owes nothing to a *Deus ex machina*, but eveything to the Spirit inside the man, who exchanges life for death, so that death may cease its hold on life. 'All is best, though we oft doubt' echoes the chorus, and the reader ponders the last line. Can he today subscribe to 'calm of mind all passion spent'? If, as is likely, the future after these fifty years will bring all to a climacteric Samson event, so that Gaza will be incinerated together with Samson, can such an end be received, even in advance, with 'calm of mind all passion spent'?

The answer lies, of course, in the future. But it is a future which, following upon the tragedy, may also lie *Beyond Tragedy*, as Niebuhr insisted. This *beyond* is implicit in our survey. It must assume the supremacy of the Spirit and the defeat of the monolithic totalitarian lie. This lie has already been unmasked, but its power not yet undone. If the lie undoes itself, following its own methods and purposes, Samson may not have to offer himself to bring down the pillars. But our survey has shown that although events seem to move mechanically, along a course determined by economic and strategic rules, they must be appropriated by the human kind. This remains the task, if not of a Samson who buried all beneath him, of the unknown warrior of the present day. My little gallery of peaceful warriors must be joined to the innumerable host who have thus made history, as yet with a disturbed mind all passion still intact.

The faces of my period of history haunt me and inspire me, for they represent the inscrutable meaning of our destiny.

The Hitlers, Himmlers, Goebbels, Stalins, Molotovs, Vyshinskys confront the Churchills, Roosevelts, Rathenaus, Kennedys, Bonhoeffers — individual faces now attached to plural factions, symbolizing the strange affair of our times. I see behind it an uninterpreted medley of intoxication, falsehood, and torture. I discern behind this medley the unalterable order of creation, redemption, and sanctification. I now leave the machine-guns, bomb blasts, hangings, and also relinquish my hold on the elect. My final picture takes me to Johannesburg in 1961 where I lectured at the College of the Community of the Resurrection. The new laws of apartheid required the closing down of the college which had served the black community in what was now a white neighbourhood. For the last time the college doors were thrown open to former students and friends. They came for hundreds of miles, from the Transvaal, Natal, the Cape Province, and beyond. They used any transport that offered. They arrived days before the start of the festivities. The Fathers welcomed everyone and no one was without bed or food. The nuns served the community. The climax came with a Solemn Eucharist, followed by an open air banquet. All Christian denominations were present. I talked also to a man who turned out to be a spy of the police. No matter: everyone talked openly. The people sang and danced, then rested on the grass. Many children and babies were held in mothers' arms. Were there five thousand, or more? The proceedings began, and I was overtaken by that ecstasy which I had first experienced so many decades ago. Here was the light reflecting the *Beatissima Lux*: men serving and being served, spontaneously and in good order. Here all the cultures met, for Indians and Chinese could also be seen on the grass. The theme of the final farewell evoked tears and laughter. We were transfigured: it was good to be there.

Another decade has passed and many more will pass in their turn. Then we cried for the beloved country and found naught for our comfort, for things were getting worse. Violence still threatens, there on the Rand and down to the Cape of Good Hope, and thence along the ocean routes. The final *Et in terra pax hominibus bonae voluntatis* still confronts glory rendered to the state, homage exacted by tyrants, envy among men of ill will. As I write in the greenest England under a blue sky, rent by dissension, fearful of its future, the men are cutting and bringing in the harvest. First comes the hay and quite soon the corn. The cows gather to yield the milk, and the sheep graze on all the hills. Our greatest joy comes from the bees in our garden. They had a bad winter and spring offered only cold winds. But now the sun shines and all the poets seem to speak through them of hope. Unbroken is this history of true work and buzzing devotion. And when the sun sinks in the west Venus heralds the warm night, and soon all the stars radiate the Unity in myriad energies. As I look up I know what has been, though not why; and I pray that a future cosmic glory will correspond to our hopes and sufferings.

INDEX